JOE HENDERSON'S RUNNING HANDBOOK

JOE HENDERSON'S RUNNING HANDBOOK

Joe Henderson

wcb

Wm. C. Brown Publishers
Dubuque, Iowa

Books by Joe Henderson
Long, Slow Distance (1969)
Road Racers and Their Training (1970)
Thoughts on the Run (1970)
Run Gently, Run Long (1974)
The Long Run Solution (1976)
Jog, Run, Race (1977)
Run Farther, Run Faster (1979)
The Running Revolution (1980)
Running, A to Z (1983)
Running Your Best Race (1984)
Running for Fitness, for Sport,
and for Life (1984)

Cover Photo by Don Person

Illustrations by Don Person

Copyright © 1985 by Joe Henderson. All rights reserved

Library of Congress Catalog Card Number: 85–71677

Book
ISBN 0–697–00795–2

Book and Diskette
ISBN 0–697–00770–7

Printed in the United States of America
10 9 8 7 6 5 4 3 2 1

For the late Jim Fixx, who introduced millions of people to running, and was a friend of mine. He lives on in us.

Contents

Tables and Figures

Figures

Foreword

For almost as many years as I have been writing, I have been making periodic phone calls to Joe Henderson to tell him I am through, washed up. I will never again write anything worth reading.

And for just as many years, he has reassured me that all will be well. He has reminded me that I have passed innumerable such crises before, and this one, too, shall pass.

I go through the ritual because Joe is the only person I trust when it comes to writing about running. If I write one sentence, even one word, that is weak or exaggerated or untrue, he will catch it immediately. If the writing is a fraction off-key, a hair out of tune, his eye and ear will detect it. In regard to running writing, Joe has perfect pitch.

When I look for the truth about running, I read Joe Henderson. What he demands of his writing is not sincerity alone; every runner/writer seems to have that quality. It is not enough for Joe to simply tell the truth; the revelation has to delve deeper and use just the right words in doing so. What Joe strives for is veracity, which is a product of sincerity plus discipline, hard work, and the desire to use yourself up completely. Veracity has a clarity that sincerity can only hope to achieve.

Joe brings that clarity to his writing. He is a deceptively simplistic writer who makes it look easy. His instinct and intuition about the running experience give him complete control, complete confidence. As you read his work, this control becomes evident. There is the leaving unsaid of things that need not be said, the avoidance of pretense about things he doesn't know. What he knows is enough.

Henderson is the most modest writer I have ever met, the gentlest and most understanding editor. It is sufficient reward for him that he has a talent, a passion, and an opportunity to use them.

What he is uncompromising about is his writing time. He writes as he runs: seven days every week. His newsletters, magazine articles, and books are products of that daily writing and running, those excursions into his inner and outer worlds.

Joe's writings have encouraged every runner to think of him as a friend. I sometimes think of him as more like my twin. I think of my relationship with Joe as being unique, but I'm sure it isn't. Others also call him and get reassurance that all is well. Others also have that faith in his ability to determine what is first-rate and what is ordinary.

Joe Henderson, in his quiet way, has given us and our sport credibility. His writings have validated the running experience. But he has also demonstrated an even more important truth: Once you have decided that winning isn't everything, you become a winner.

George A. Sheehan, M.D.

George Sheehan, one of the best-known names in running writing, serves as medical editor for Runner *magazine and has authored several well-known volumes on the sport.*

Preface

"Most of my writing is an unconscionable self-indulgence, because for the most part I have written about things I love. Fundamentally I am a very happy person. I have been lucky enough to find a way of making a living while doing what I want to be doing anyway, and what I would do even if I didn't have to make a living."

Jim Fixx spoke those words to fellow running writer Amby Burfoot shortly before Fixx's death. He lived happily because his work and his hobby were one and the same. By that definition, I, too, am a happy and lucky man who earns a living at what I once did (and may someday do again) for nothing.

I've written about running for almost as long as I've been running (which is twenty-seven years), and still write as often as I run (which is daily). The two activities have been inseparable since the 1950s, so I obviously feel the same way about running as writing. Fundamentally, I am a very happy runner who once earned tangible rewards from racing, but who has long since quit getting or needing them.

The writing is only incidental to this book. The words are merely a medium for expressing ideas gathered during my years on the road. My credits as a writer aren't the credentials that count the most here. In this context, I'm a runner who happens to write, not a writer who happens to run. I try speak to you as one runner to another, not as author to reader. I suggest nothing to you here that I haven't done or wouldn't do myself.

My major qualification is that I have survived. I've made all the mistakes, corrected most of them, and in the process learned some lessons on lasting and some lasting lessons. These I share with you now, in the hope that your mistakes are fewer and your lessons more quickly learned than mine.

Survival isn't a consolation prize. It's a runner's greatest victory. Trophies tarnish, records fall, youth fades. What lasts is the running itself. You win again each day simply by wanting to and being able to keep running, by staying healthy, eager, and active.

How much I run each day is unspectacular. It averages little more than half an hour, usually at a comfortable pace. At this rate, I don't outrun many people. But I've *outlasted* quite a few.

I once wrote, "The challenge in running is not to aim at doing what no one else has done, but to keep doing what anyone could do. It's harder sometimes to keep going back over the same ground you've covered thousands of times before than to go someplace you've never been. It's harder to get down to the little, everyday tasks than to get up for the big, special ones. I'm proudest of the little things I've done in running."

Those words went into a book written nearly a decade ago, during the early rumblings of what came to be known as the "running boom." At that time, I'd run my modest way for some 6000 days. The count has now grown to almost 10,000 days. The little efforts have added up to something big and still expanding. Meanwhile, faster, harder-working runners continue to come into the sport—and go out of it.

Watching their comings and goings gives me no sense of superiority or satisfaction. I'd prefer to see more runners last longer because appreciation of this activity ripens with age.

With that goal in mind, I offer you these thoughts and techniques from a lifetime on the road. The ideas and practices expressed and explained here have withstood tests of time. That's the only claim I make, or feel I need to make, for this material.

Joe Henderson
Eugene, Oregon

JOE HENDERSON'S RUNNING HANDBOOK

P A R T   O N E

THE RUNNING EXPERIENCE

*I*f you like public floggings, you'd love the review process for a book. The author stands defenseless before the critics, absorbing their blows without being allowed to cry out in pain or anger.

As an author, I'd lived a rather sheltered life. I'd preached to a limited congregation of already converted runners who forgave my lapses in fact and style. The rare reviews had generally been kind, probably because the reviewers were friends. Those who had nothing good to say had simply said nothing.

All that changed with the book published before this one, a text for college activity courses. Publishers in this market deal with skeptical academicians whose criticisms must be anticipated before the book reaches print.

Each author bares his manuscript to a pre-publication review board made up of experts from the field. These people are truth-seekers by nature and are paid to question whether what is written is true or not. Their comments are tough. Nothing personal, you understand. These are what a scientist might call "double-blind" reviews. The reviewers aren't told who wrote the book, and the author doesn't know his critics. Only facts and style are up for discussion, not personalities. The result is a better book for all.

These thoughts didn't soothe me as I stared at the thick, ominous-looking envelope that I'd hoped would never come. It held the six anonymous reviews.

"What if I just throw it away and pretend it never came?" I wondered. "What if I don't read the reviews and just tell the editor, 'I don't agree with any of the suggestions, and if you want revisions then our deal is off'?"

Then I recalled advice given by an old journalism professor: "If you voluntarily become a stripper, don't complain about the working conditions."

My job is to bare my thoughts in public. If the crowd boos, those are the working conditions I must accept.

I read the reviews and found them to be mixed. They ranged from "Some of the best material ever written on the subject" to "Superficial and simplistic; totally unsuitable for a college-level course." Those statements cancelled each other.

One reviewer wrote with unintended humor. He said, "This book is inferior to the one we now use in our running classes." He listed its author as Joe Henderson.

Most of the suggested changes vastly improved the book. But other comments echoing through the reviews seemed to challenge the very ground upon which I run. For instance, I flatly stated:

- "The perfect run lasts between thirty and sixty minutes."
- "The ideal training pace is a minute or two per mile slower than racing pace."
- "The safe speed limit is ten percent of total mileage."
- "The easiest way to increase mileage is by taking walking breaks."
- "The best way to warm up is by running slowly, not by stretching."

The experts responded with statements such as, "This recommendation is contradicted by the research," and, "Quote a reference."

I can't quote what I haven't read. I didn't study this material. I *lived* it, experimenting with it and refining it during my long tenure at the University of the Roads. I'm a pragmatist who uses whatever works.

These reviewers are scientists, and I fancy myself an artist. They are trained in the scientific method, which demands proof of every statement. I rely on instincts and experiences that can't be quantified. I believe in magic.

People who live by the numbers may have a hard time accepting another claim of mine: that most of the "rules" guiding runners still defy logical explanation. The more I learn about running, the less sure I am that there are any final answers, the less sure I am of what I definitely know.

I don't try to explain everything. I accept certain experiences as illogical, but nonetheless real and true.

The Progress

I'm not a historian; I'm merely an observer and a reporter. At the risk of oversimplifying a much bigger story, these are my nominations as the trends, inventions, techniques, and ideas that have done the most to advance the sport during my running lifetime.

Running Magazines

I speak here not as a magazine person but as someone whose early interest was nurtured almost solely by reading matter. As a boy in rural Iowa, I rarely saw other runners. My interest in the sport would have shriveled and died if not for magazines that told me I wasn't alone.

Bert and Cordner Nelson's *Track and Field News* sparked that interest, but it was and is a magazine about the elite runner we'd like to be. Browning Ross's *Long Distance Log* sustained my interest because it dealt with the type of runner most of us really are: the mid-pack participant.

Long Distance Log served as the only link among the country's isolated road runners from 1956 through the mid-1960s. Long before *Runner's World* was conceived, Ross labored alone at his home in New Jersey, telling us what was happening in the sport. His magazine was never fancy and rarely was published on time, but the few hundred subscribers lucky enough to know of *LDL* studied it more eagerly than anything we read now.

Ross showed us that there was more to running than circling the track a few times. He showed a few of us what was going on in the sport before there were enough of us to support a more professional magazine. Several of Ross's readers would go on to publish, edit, and write for the bigger magazines that followed. They continued his work of giving individual runners a sense of community.

Running Books

At the same time Browning Ross was reporting what distance runners were doing, Fred Wilt was telling us how to do it. His first book, *How They Train,* allowed him to coach thousands of runners he never met.

Wilt was my first coach, even though we still haven't met. In the late 1950s, I read *How They Train* until its pages fell out. Hundreds of other runners first learned training techniques from that little orange masterpiece.

Long-distance running grew up outside the structure of high school and college teams. Few runners had coaches in the 1950s and 1960s (or have them now), so they created a demand for books that provided indirect coaching. Arthur Lydiard passed along the principles of a training revolution in *Run to the Top.* Kenneth Cooper, M.D., later guided millions of people into running for exercise with his book, *Aerobics.*

Finally, Jim Fixx tied together the expanding body of technical know-how for a growing number of runners. His *Complete Book of Running* may not have been the best book ever written on this subject, but it came at the right time. Thousands of people now think of Fixx as their first coach.

U.S. Success

Frank Shorter is widely credited with lighting the fuse that led to the running explosion in the United States. His marathon victory at the 1972 Olympics did have an enormous impact, but Shorter wasn't the first American to succeed at that level.

Through the early 1960s, U.S. distance runners were the joke of international track meets, usually straggling home a lap behind the winners of the 5000 and 10,000 meters. No American had ever won an Olympic race at these distances. Observers in this country and abroad speculated that this was a nation of speed and strength; its athletes had no staying power, no patience, no will to put in the hard work required of a distance runner.

No runner is more American than Billy Mills. He was born on an Indian reservation in South Dakota, was schooled in Kansas, and later was an officer in the Marine Corps. Mills showed that no one could laugh at American Olympians any more. He showed, too, that a runner could succeed at both a track race and the marathon at the same time. Mills competed well on the road at the Tokyo Olympics after his stunning upset victory in the 10,000. Eight years later, Shorter would do well in the 10,000 before winning the marathon.

By then, thanks also to Tokyo 5000 gold medalist Bob Schul and world-record marathoner Buddy Edelen, our national inferiority complex had vanished.

Training Shifts

It's the nature of runners to think that if one of something is good, two of it must be twice as good. Interval training, a method with important uses, was being abused in the 1950s. Runners were taking too much of it too often.

Arthur Lydiard weaned his New Zealand athletes away from excessive track intervals and put them on high-mileage road training. Peter Snell and Murray Halberg responded with gold medals at the 1960s Olympics. The running world responded to that success by switching from interval-based to distance-based programs—sometimes erring by doing too much of *that* too often.

Lydiard's main contribution was 100-mile weeks; those were but a piece of his gift to the sport. His more important message was that training must be balanced. He first had to eliminate wasteful speedwork. Later, when revisionists of his theories tipped the scales too heavily toward slow distance, he warned that they were equally unbalanced in the opposite direction.

Bill Bowerman, America's coaching genius, preached another kind of balance: between work and rest. He said that no one becomes a better runner without working, but no one improves by working hard all the time, either.

More than twenty years ago, Bowerman promoted the idea that waves of hard and easy effort are basic to any successful running program. He said, "I'd rather see a runner underwork than overwork." Only in recent years, as injury rates have grown to epidemic proportions, have runners recognized the wisdom of those words. We're finally moving away from mile-counting and bragging about how much suffering we can tolerate toward relaxation without guilt between big efforts.

Running as Exercise

Until the late 1960s, running was purely and simply a sport. Kenneth Cooper made it an exercise. His research as an Air Force physician had convinced him of the link between regular endurance activity and good health, and he taught the world the meaning of the word *aerobic*.

Cooper wrote neither a running book nor a jogging book. *Aerobics*, published in 1968, was an exercise text, listing running as one option among many. He didn't mention the word *jogging;* that was someone else's creation.

Still, the message of this longtime runner was clear: Cooper favored running as a fitness activity. At the time, running as sport was thought to be weird, but anything done in the name of looking lean and helping the heart was becoming fashionable.

Of the millions of people who began running to work off flab and improve their plumbing, tens of thousands stayed with it for other reasons: relaxation, recreation, competition. Cooper inspired people to start running for their lives, and in the process led many of them into a lifetime of running.

Road Racing

Kenneth Cooper's exercise and Arthur Lydiard's training came together in road racing. This most democratic of sports offered a meeting place for runners moving up from fitness and down from serious competition on the track.

Cooper's converts found they liked running enough to want more of it. Lydiard's disciples enjoyed road training so much that they wanted to move into road racing. The two groups blended to produce and promote two unique aspects of road races: the "everyone's-a-winner" philosophy and the "fun-run" approach.

During the "Me Decade" of the 1970s, we learned to take pride in ourselves and what we can do. Rather than watch athletes perform, we *became* athletes. Rather than look up to heroes, we made heroes of ourselves. We adopted the attitude that to participate is to win, to improve a personal record is to win bigger, and the only way to lose is to give up.

Running isn't always fun, but winning is. The races in which everyone had a chance to feel like a winner became happy occasions. These celebrations of self became events shared with hundreds or even thousands of fellow celebrants.

Running for All

One person can open up opportunities for whole groups of people. Two who did that were Kathrine Switzer as a leader of women and David Pain with his early work on behalf of older runners.

The Switzer legend has grown with women's running, and the details of her confrontation with officialdom at the 1967 Boston Marathon are well known and frequently repeated. I add just two points: Switzer is a pioneer not for running Boston first (Roberta Gibb had finished in 1966), but for challenging—innocently, she claims—the rule barring women from racing with men.

Switzer didn't stop there. A lively woman with an instinct for promotion, she became a mother figure in the ultimately successful crusade for international marathoning equality. Maybe it takes a P. T. Barnum-type to put momentum into any movement. Switzer's promotional talents certainly got the women's marathon moving toward Olympic acceptance.

David Pain did the same for the Masters, although running for men in their forties and older wasn't his invention. Many of them hadn't known when to quit, and still competed in long-distance races in the 1960s. But they rarely raced for prizes against runners their own age. Track athletes of that age group rarely could compete at all.

Then came Pain. The pilot, lawyer, promoter, handball player, and miler sometimes lived up to his last name, hounding track meet directors in California to include mile races for runners over forty. The directors relented, as much to get Pain off their backs as to create a new branch of the sport.

Pain is gone from the sport now, off on some new crusade. He left in a huff, complaining that "politics" had driven him out. More likely, running lost its excitement for him. A revolutionary loses interest once the fight is won.

Scientific Scrutiny

Much of what we thought we knew about running in the 1960s has been labeled as wrong by scientists who accept nothing on faith. The leader of the myth-killers has been David Costill, Ph.D., operating out of the Human Performance Laboratory at Ball State University. He first translated the findings of exercise physiology into practical terms in the landmark booklet, *What Research Tells the Coach about Distance Running.*

Before Costill and others put the sport under scrutiny, runners ate steak and eggs "for strength" before competition. We refused to drink water during a race or while training, thinking it would cause cramps. Costill's studies proved conclusively that fluid restriction harms performance and that drinking helps. He and his sports medicine colleagues campaigned successfully for more frequent aid stations on race courses, and educated runners about the need to drink.

Scandinavian scientists reported that a runner's primary source of fuel is glycogen, a product of starchy and sugary foods. The scientists' research showed that increased carbohydrate intake improves endurance, while overloading with proteins and fats can have the opposite effect. Almost everyone now practices some form of carbohydrate-loading before long-distances races, if only because these foods taste so good.

Preventive Medicine

George Sheehan, a physician himself, once wrote that runners have three natural enemies: dogs, drivers, and doctors. He named the last group because doctors' attitudes toward running injuries ranged from indifference to ignorance. The standard prescription they offered an injured runner was, "Stop running."

That was symptomatic treatment, and the symptoms usually returned as soon as the running was resumed. Fortunately, doctors are now treating the causes of our complaints, thereby working toward permanent cures. The two major medical advances have been biomechanical control and supplementary exercises.

Podiatrists have become the first line of defense against injury and the first specialists many runners turn to when injured. Among the pioneers at controlling injuries by controlling footplant were Richard Schuster, D.P.M., on the east coast, and Steven Subotnick, D.P.M., on the west.

The person who specializes in running to the exclusion of all other physical activity is an endangered species. Yoga-like stretching exercises for injury prevention gained popularity in the 1970s. In the 1980s, significant numbers of runners began adopting weight training to balance their muscle development. People who'll never race a triathlon have added bicycling and swimming as supplements to their running or as substitutes when they can't run.

Material Needs

What we'd like to think of as the most natural of sports has received a major boost from synthetic products: nylon, Gore-Tex, polypropylene, lycra, plastic. . . . The list of high-tech materials goes on and on.

The Japanese company, Tiger, started a shoemaking revolution in the late 1960s by introducing the now-universal nylon upper. This innovation, along with softer soles and better heel support, took some of the pain out of running long distances on hard surfaces.

Frank Shorter first marketed a light, comfortable, attractive nylon rainsuit, and Bill Rodgers soon followed Shorter's lead. Gore-Tex suits and polypro and lycra tights have supplied a near-cure for the common cold.

The lightweight plastic digital watch has become a portable computer at an abacus-like price. Seiko introduced digitals in the mid-1970s at a cost of hundreds of dollars. Since then, competition and improved methods of mass production have provided the rarest of combinations: higher quality at a small fraction of the original price.

CHAPTER TWO

The Questions

Questions. They are the pulse of a writer's life. Interviews in which questions are asked and answered provide my raw material for stories, of course. But the questions people ask *me* are just as important a source. These queries let me know what runners are wanting to know.

The questions asked, and answered briefly, in this chapter form recurring themes. They serve as an introduction to longer answers given later in the book.

"I have this friend who wants to start running. What are the most important things I should tell her?"

Not many would-be runners read me, so most beginners must get this answer second-hand—from a friend who already runs. My advice is drawn almost word for word from Kenneth Cooper, M.D.

Go immediately to three miles or thirty minutes, whichever comes first, and stay there. Repeat the session at least every other day. Walk some, most, or all of this distance or time if that's the only way to finish it comfortably.

Dr. Cooper, the man generally credited with putting America on the road to aerobic fitness, is not a fanatical runner. Although he ran in high school and college, and has exercised this way for more than twenty years, he claims he doesn't even particularly enjoy running. But he likes the results it gives him for a limited time investment. Cooper's typical run lasts considerably less than thirty minutes, and he has mountains of data to prove that this is enough to maintain physical fitness.

He writes in *The Aerobics Program for Total Well-Being:* "Recent research has shown that unless a person is training for marathons or other competitive events, it's best to limit running to around twelve to fifteen miles per week. More than that will greatly increase the incidence of joint and bone injuries, and other ailments. On the other hand, less mileage will fail to achieve the desired improvement in the body."

Cooper and his staff at the Aerobics Center in Dallas have been "overwhelmed" by the injury rates in people running more than twenty-five miles a week. While a competitor may willingly take the risks associated with higher mileage, Cooper says it first yields diminishing returns and eventually negative ones. For non-racers, he sets minimums and maximums: no less than two miles, four days a week, and no more than three miles on five days.

An overrated rule: *Grow fit by running more miles.* Fitter for what? For marathons, perhaps, but not fitter in the general-health sense. Cooper says, "If you run more than fifteen miles a week, you're running for something other than fitness."

"How much mileage should I be putting in if I'm training for races ten kilometers and up? I've heard you need to run at least 10-K each day to get any benefits."

Oh, how distance has been devalued when we think that anything less than six miles a day does no good! I suspect it is about the *farthest* most of us should run most of the time.

We run for more than thirty minutes because we run for more than fitness—which, as George Sheehan, M.D., says, "is a stage you pass through on the way to becoming an athlete." The sport begins where the exercise ends: at about the half-hour mark. But few runners need repeated runs longer than an hour, and few can even tolerate them.

Training for races is hard work. It involves some runs at the speed of the shortest race and some at the distance of the longest one. Precisely for that reason, the running routine must also involve lots of easy runs for recovery between the hard ones. We don't recover overnight, and we delay that healing by trying to put in too many miles at the wrong time.

An article in the British magazine *Running* addresses the question: What are the recovery rates from various amounts of running? Ron Maughan reviews a study from Holland which examined degrees of muscle damage. Because human runners balk at having their muscles dissected, the researchers used rats as their subjects.

Maughan writes that "the exercise intensity was not severe and would correspond to a fairly moderate training session [in humans]. The first conclusion was that thirty-minute runs on a treadmill caused no visible problem, while sixty-minute sessions produced marked signs of muscle damage."

"Interestingly," says Maughan, "there are few signs of muscle degeneration in the immediate post-exercise [sixty-minute run] period. Signs of damage became apparent only after a few hours had elapsed, and appeared to be most pronounced after twenty-four to forty-eight hours had elapsed." This may explain the delayed stiffness we feel a day or two after a long race or training run.

Maughan reports that recovery began in the third day and that "all signs of change which were observed appeared to be reversible."

A second overrated rule: *Run better by building a larger mileage base.* The weekly mileage count may be the least important, most misleading figure in a runner's diary. This counting causes us to run too much on days we should be easing off, and tires us too much to run enough on days that should be long and fast. Big *days* are what count most, not big weeks. Make those days good and hard, and then make the rest of the week nice and easy.

"I've been running for a while, have finished a few 10-K's, and now I want to try a marathon. What kind of training should I do?"

This was the number-one question a few years ago and still ranks near the top. Review these two key points.

- Add one long run a week. This is the foundation of Jeff Galloway's marathon training plan, the one I now recommend to first-timers. Galloway advises increasing the long run until it totals full marathon distance. Equally important are the minimum-distance recovery runs that occupy all the days between long efforts.
- Run longer by walking. This is Tom Osler's idea. He says runners can increase their distances quickly and safely by inserting walking breaks of perhaps five minutes every half-hour. Using the Osler technique, a runner might aim first at training a full marathon by using these "intervals," and then by eliminating all or most of the walks on race day.

A third overrated rule: *Run every step of every training session.* Osler has shown how we can double the length of runs, without doubling the effort, through selective walking.

"I seem to be stuck on a plateau where my times aren't improving. How can I race faster?"

This appears to be the most frequently asked question today. A friend came to me with this familiar lament. The thrill had gone out of racing as her times had stagnated. "What can I do to get better?" she asked.

My first answer was to run short races, in the five-kilometer range. Racing is the most specific and most exciting form of speed training.

"But this is winter," she replied, "and we don't have any of those events scheduled now."

As an alternative, I recommended a fast mile on the track once a week. Split the mile into its four laps, and walk a lap in between. Time only the running portion, and try to go at least a minute and not more than two minutes faster than the normal per-mile running pace.

After just four weeks of training this way, my friend improved her long-plateaued 10-K race time by nearly three minutes. Improvements of almost thirty seconds per mile are rare gifts, but a drop of at least ten seconds per mile is not too much to expect from this small amount of speed training applied by someone who has done none before.

A fourth overrated rule: *Improve speed by running faster all the time.* A little bit of speed training goes a long way, without taking the physical and psychological toll of constant speeding.

"The race is tomorrow morning. What final advice can you give me for making it go smoother and faster?"

I hear this question first at pre-race clinics, when the training die already has been cast but jittery runners still look for a final edge. I tell them they might find it by practicing restraint.

You might finish faster, I suggest, by starting slower. Even if you've done everything right in training, you can cancel all that good with as little as one wrong move on race day. The first and worst bad move is leaving the starting line too quickly.

Check your watch at the midpoint, I continue, and then again at the finish. Compare your first- and second-half splits. The times should be almost equal.

A fifth overrated rule: *The way to set a personal record is to go out hard and "put time in the bank" early, allowing for the inevitable slowdown later on.* Records are broken by maintaining pace in the first half of the race. Hearts are broken by starting too fast.

"What and when should I eat before a race?"

The only pre-race diet better than carbohydrate-loading may be no food at all. So say researchers from East Carolina University. Ron Maughan, the science columnist for *Running* magazine, reviews the findings from a study on rats:

"The authors of this report showed that treadmill-running endurance capacity can be increased if preceded by a twenty-four-hour fast. The fast resulted in low values of blood glucose, and also decreased the liver and muscle glycogen stores. In view of the well-recognized importance of these carbohydrate stores in determining the ability to perform prolonged exercise, the increase in endurance capacity seems somewhat paradoxical.

"However, in spite of the fact that resting glycogen levels were lower in the fasted animals, the glycogen content in skeletal muscle after the run to exhaustion was *higher* in the fasted than the fed rats. There was no difference in liver glycogen content at exhaustion between the fed and fastest groups."

A glycogen-sparing effect was taking place, says Maughan, and another energy-producing substance was being recruited more heavily. While these results may not translate into human terms, Maughan notes, they "may call for a re-examination of the use of carbohydrate-loading diets by marathon runners."

While I stop short of recommending a full twenty-four-hour fast, I would say there is little to be gained from eating during those hours.

A sixth overrated rule: *Load with carbohydrates shortly before racing.* As many races are lost by carbo-loading improperly as are won by doing it correctly. The depletion phase is particularly risky because confidence and resistance to illness deplete along with energy. The loading itself can also cause difficulties. As race time approaches, more problems arise from feeling too full than from running on empty.

"What is the value to a runner of other exercises and other sports? Weights? Stretching?"

Don't think of the extras as requirements. If you like to lift and stretch, exercise those options. But take them in the right amounts and for the right reasons. The amounts shouldn't cut into running time and energy. The reasons have little to do with improvement as a runner.

Running itself is a form of weight training, since you lift your body weight about 1500 times per mile. The legs, therefore, don't require much additional attention. And adding upper-body strength yields little measurable benefit in terms of running performance. So why should you think about strength at all?

In a word, *balance*. Running's effects on the upper body are nil, so if you don't want to end up looking as flabby as a plucked chicken, you might want to adopt the habit of regular strength-building.

The simplest, yet still quite effective, exercises are old-fashioned pushups and situps. Standard pushups and bent-leg situps, whatever number you can tolerate, will keep you respectably strong on a time investment of just a few minutes a day.

Stretching exercises are not, as commonly supposed and practiced, intended for warming up before a run. You can warm up better and faster by running slowly for the first mile or so. Stretching is meant to counteract the tightening effects of the run, and is therefore best practiced during mid-run breaks or immediately after finishing. The muscles respond best to stretching after they have been warmed.

Five minutes a day will keep you as loose as a runner needs to be. You're not training for ballet.

A seventh overrated rule: *Stretch diligently to prevent injuries.* One study on stretching's effects gives little comfort to stretchers. Results from the Honolulu Marathon Clinic indicate that runners who stretch get hurt *more often* than those who avoid these exercises. This could be because people are stretching the wrong way. Like training, extra exercise is a prescription item that can be misused and overdosed.

"I'm injured, and no cure I've tried has helped. How can I get rid of the problem so I can run normally again?"

Not being able to run normally, or at all, hurts worse than the injury itself. An injured runner may react irrationally by going to one extreme or the other: either trying to run through the injury and delaying recovery, or stopping all physical activity and slipping badly out of shape.

The rational course of rehabilitiation steers between all and nothing. A runner can work through almost any injury.

World champion trackman Eamonn Coghlan, a frequent victim of injuries, said while recovering from a stress fracture, "People think that when you're not running, you're not training. Well, right now I'm training as hard [through other activities] in terms of cardio-vascular and strength work as I would be if I were competing. I haven't missed a day of training all winter."

Joan Benoit missed hardly any training after undergoing arthroscopic knee surgery in April 1984. She worked out furiously on a bicycle while waiting to resume running. Less than three weeks later, she won the Olympic Trials Marathon.

By substituting the other two activities of the triathlon for the missing one during the recovery period, a runner loses very little conditioning. More important, he or she doesn't suffer the pangs of withdrawal that go with forced rest.

An eighth overrated rule: *Rest is the only cure for most running injuries.* Total rest is hardly ever required. If you can't run steadily without pain, you still may be able to mix running and walking. If you can't run/walk, bike. If you can't bike, swim. Anything is better than nothing.

"All the advertising claims about shoes only confuse me. Is there anything new on the market that I should try?"

The trend in shoemaking has been toward *more:* more padding, more support, more stability, more lift. A legendary New Zealander marathoner, however, makes a good case for wearing less.

Jack Foster has put more than twenty years of hard running on his legs, including a 2:11 marathon at age forty-one. Conventional wisdom insists that older bodies need more protection. Yet Foster prefers the least of all shoes.

"I was introduced to running over farmlands, where the underfoot conditions were soft and unyielding, and one developed good strength and flexibility," he says. "I ran in light tennis shoes, because there were no training shoes in those days."

Jack thinks those shoes forced him to learn proper running style. "We ran in those flimsy, light shoes and developed a 'feel' for the ground. We learned to land properly or got sore legs, since we couldn't rely on the shoes to absorb any shock. We got into a light-footed gait, which moved us over hill and dale very effectively. I'm certain this [running style] helped me stay injury-free."

Even now, when shoe companies beg him to wear their latest high-tech training flats, Foster says, "I continue to run daily in shoes most people consider too light even for racing."

A ninth overrated rule: *Provide the feet with the most protection that money can buy.* Just the opposite may be true. You may not go all the way to the Foster extreme, but you might profit by choosing the least shoe you can tolerate.

"I'm in my forties and still want to improve my racing performances. Am I too old to be thinking about that?"

Calendar age means little. What counts is your running age. I am old in my forties—more than a quarter-century and 50,000 miles old in the ways that really matter: the amount of time and mileage I've put on my legs. You're still an infant in your forties if you've only recently begun to race. You probably can look forward to many years of improvement.

Joan Ullyot, M.D., author of *Women's Running,* wrote a "Rule of Ten" which appears to be generally valid (though I might reduce the number slightly): "You won't reach your full potential as an athlete until you have trained for about ten years."

Runners adapt slowly and steadily to the stresses of racing, she says, and improvement usually continues for years on even modest amounts of consistent training. The beauty of this rule of thumb is that the clock doesn't start ticking until the runner begins competing.

Even after that period expires, says Jack Foster, who now runs marathons a half-minute per mile slower than he did at his best, "The drop-off in racing performances manifests itself only on timekeepers' stopwatches. The running action, the breathing, and the other experiences of racing all feel the same."

A tenth overrated rule: *Distance runners peak in their mid- to late-twenties.* The sport's best runners usually are drawn from that age group. But it would be wrong to assume that individual runners outside that range have no hope of improving. You can expect five to ten good years of improvement, no matter whether you start at age five or fifty-five.

The Secrets

The more I run and write about it, the less certain I am of what I really know. The more I learn, the less sure I am that there are any absolute answers. The more I practice the sport, the less accepting I am of "accepted" practices. The more I read and hear, the less likely I am to believe what experts write and say.

The years on the road have let me in on many of running's best-kept secrets. Experience has taught me a lot, but above all it has shown me that no one can ever know everything about anything. I introduce you to what I *think* I know in this chapter and admit to not knowing all. Some of it defies conventional theory. Read it both openly and critically.

The Running Experience

Running is not "fun." The act of running isn't, anyway—at least not in the ha-ha sense. "Satisfying" is a better description. Running gives the type of quiet satisfaction felt by an artist in the act of creating.

It isn't satisfying every day. Some days you feel so-so; others days, downright awful. But you wade through those days to reach the one or two a week that satisfy you.

Running is an art form. It fits the broad definition of art as making something where nothing existed before, of making something special and personal from common ingredients available to all.

Runners don't often smile while running, for the same reasons that artists don't look happy while at work. They are concentrating on their demanding task of creating. In your case, you're building an ability that didn't exist before you began to run.

Running is an investment, not an expense. It doesn't cost time and energy; it *earns* them by making you more organized and efficient in the other hours of the day.

Running is a natural laxative. There may be no such thing as a "runner's high," but the "non-runner's low" is very real and something we run to avoid. Running flushes out the wastes accumulated while sitting still and lets you feel as good as a moving body should.

"The loneliness of the long-distance runner" is no problem. The rare chance to be alone, away from the voices and thoughts of others, is one of running's main attractions.

You can be your own hero. What you run should be more important than anything that happens to the superstars of the sport. Other people may run farther and faster, but no one can do your running for you or take away what you have done.

The Running Body (Medicine)

You are responsible for your own health. Doctors are responsible only for correcting serious injuries and illnesses. Their job is to practice medicine. Yours is to practice prevention.

Most running ailments are self-inflicted. You don't *get* injured; you injure yourself, usually by running too far, too fast, too often. You don't *catch* colds and the flu; they catch you when you drop your resistance.

Pain is a friend to be heeded, not a foe to be fought or ignored. It is friendly warning that something is wrong. If you pay attention to your pain, you can stop the damage at its source. Enduring pain doesn't equal gain. It adds up to more and more pain, until all running must cease.

Few running ailments are serious when judged by the standards of football knees or ski ankles. Most running problems cause only localized pain, and very few of them are permanent.

Time is the best healer and the only treatment required for most running ailments. Six weeks will cure most injuries, provided the stress that caused the problem is reduced or eliminated.

Everyone needs a big injury. It shows what running really means to you and teaches you better lessons about injury-prevention than any author or speaker ever could.

The Running Body (Diet)

You burn the same number of calories per mile while running easily as you do by running hard. So if your main goal is to lose weight, slow down and go longer.

The greatest immediate value of vegetarian and high-fiber/low-fat diets (of the Nathan Pritikin and Robert Haas type) is that they reduce weight quickly and keep it low. Gaining weight while eating only these foods is almost impossible.

Lighter weight usually means faster races. But you may feel healthier and happier while carrying a few extra pounds. They give some protection against injuries and illnesses.

Weight loss is sometimes misleading. For instance, dropping two or more pounds in one day usually means you're dehydrated, and that is never healthy.

Instead of carbohydrate-loading before a race, *reload* afterward. Carbos are both more necessary when you're depleted and more fun to eat when you don't have to worry about the side-effects of a binge.

The most effective drink before, during, and after running is plain water. It gets into the system most quickly and with the fewest complications.

The Running Environment

Mornings can be dangerous. People who jump right out of bed and into their runs are most often injured. Let the body wake up and loosen up before asking it to work hard.

Noon may be the perfect time for a working person to run. It provides a break in the workday routine, and it takes the place of a heavy lunch.

The greatest danger facing runners is the automobile. Always yield to them, regardless of what the law says. Always imagine that every driver is out to run you down.

Don't be too proud to drive to a running site. You miss most of the prettiest, quietest, and safest places by always starting and finishing at home.

Training courses are usually short. That's because you usually measure them by car, which can't cut corners like a runner does. Point-to-point courses are the most interesting but the least practical, since you must somehow get back from Point B to Point A. Lap courses are the most practical but the least exciting, since you cover the same ground repeatedly.

On a course with equal rises and descents, you never gain as much going down a hill as you lose going up. Uphills are harder to run, but downhills hurt more; the pounding stress doubles on downward slopes.

The temperature always feels warmer than it is. That's because the body is a good furnace but a poor air conditioner. This keeps you comfortable on most winter days, even if you dress rather lightly, but makes you miserable through much of the summer no matter how much clothing you take off.

Dogs are natural cowards. Stand up to them: growl and bark back, and they'll back down. Don't try to run from them, because that invites an attack from the rear.

The Running Consumer

Most runners wear too much. They dress too warmly (not to mention expensively) for the day. They wear shoes that are too heavy for their needs.

The rule of thumb for both clothing and shoes is to wear the least you can get by with, not the most you can tolerate (or afford). It's better to underdress than to overdress.

Today's shoes are made for road running. They neutralize the hard surface. Their support and cushioning qualities are excellent. But these same properties make them difficult to use on rough, off-road surfaces. The low-tech shoes of yesteryear may work better there.

Shoe weight has little to do with how heavy they feel. Solid shoes can run "light," and light ones can feel bulky. Shoes wear from the inside out as well as the outside in. Repairing the outer surface may not correct the shoe's acquired defects.

Clothes neutralize the weather. Keep the head and hands warm on cold days, dry on wet days, and you feel cozy all over. Keep the head and neck cool on hot days, and you can better tolerate the heat.

The first great running book was Arthur Lydiard's *Run to the Top;* authors are still repeating its messages. The best-kept secret in book publishing is Tom Osler's *Serious Runner's Handbook* —a masterpiece of simple wisdom and readable writing.

The oldest of magazines, *Track and Field News,* remains the standard-setter for authoritative information. Long-distance running could use a news magazine of this quality and integrity.

The Running Exercise

Most runners aren't fit in the ways all-around fitness is usually measured. Running is a specialized, incomplete exercise yielding only one-dimensional fitness. Most runners don't care if they're all-around fit or not, as long as they can run far and fast.

Running isn't the perfect exercise. If it's only exercise you want, some combination of walking, swimming, and bicycling will give similar results with less effort.

Running is more than an exercise; it is an experience. Doing it only for exercise is as limiting as eating only to strengthen the jaw muscles.

Stretching is not a warm-up exercise. It is meant to counteract the tightening effects of the run, and therefore is best done during a mid-run break or after running.

Strength training doesn't make you a better runner. But it does make you a better-balanced person by working muscles that are along for the ride when you run.

Run silently and run tall. Find a form that allows you to run without being heard. Run *over* the ground—not *on* it. Lift from the knees and spring with the ankles; don't shuffle and scuff along with the feet.

The Running Basics

Remedial running takes time. Plan to spend one month getting back into shape for every year spent slipping out of condition.

Don't run too far. The optimum fitness-running distances are two to three miles, or time periods of fifteen to thirty minutes. Little is to be gained physically from going farther.

Don't run too fast. Running at a pace that leaves you breathless contributes nothing to aerobic fitness because you are no longer running aerobically. Finish the prescribed distances comfortably, even if that requires mixing running with walking at first.

Don't run too often. Mixing hard days and easy days is a basic technical concept in running. In the early stages, any day of running is hard, so it should be followed by a day of rest.

The Running Routine

Running, training, and racing are very different activities. Running is relaxed, comfortably paced, and can be done daily. Training rehearses the speed or distance of the race without taking racing's stresses full-force. Racing goes to the limits of speed and endurance. Both must be done sparingly.

The "run" is the meat and potatoes (beans and rice, if you're a vegetarian) of the running routine. It should occupy about ninety percent of the total running time. The perfect run lasts thirty to sixty minutes. The perfect pace is one to two minutes per mile slower than the 10-K racing rate.

The hardest part of any run is the first step out the door. The hardest mile is usually the first one. You should feel less, not more, tired as you warm up. You should feel better at the end of most runs than you did at the start.

Trust your instincts. Let them, rather than a rigid schedule, guide when, where, how much, and how fast you run. Don't listen to your body at the start and let it dictate what to do. The body is a notorious liar then, looking for any excuse to do nothing. Treat the first mile or two as a gentle warm-up and a lie detector. The body will now tell you which problems are real and which were imaginary.

The Running Training

Racing is an unnatural act. You must prepare for it by doing unnatural activities. That means sometimes running farther, faster, or both, than nature intended.

Extra-long runs, speedwork, and races are prescription items. They can help or hurt, depending on their dosage. Every dose of excessive effort must be followed by several doses of easier, more natural running. The secret to making the hard work *work* is the recovery interval afterward.

Everyone knows the ingredients of training: going far enough (the speed of the shortest race but at a reduced distance), fast enough (the length of the longest race but at a reduced pace) and easy enough in between. The secret to success is knowing how to combine these three into a proper recipe.

You can prepare for a marathon on as little as thirty miles a week, provided one weekly training session mimics the marathon in length. You can prepare for a 10-K on as little as one speed session a week, provided that training mimics the 10-K in pace.

Walking breaks within the training session add to the effectiveness of this work in both distance and speed. Think of the breaks as an application of the interval system.

The Running Competition

You may have a good time at the biggest races, but you'll *run* your best times at the smaller ones. Save your big efforts for the small, well-conducted events.

If you want to race well, you should race often. Racing is the best form of speed and distance "training." If you race regularly, and over a wide variety of distances, you need little or no special training in between.

A little terror is a good thing to feel before racing. It means your mind is readying your body to go beyond its normal limits.

Most runners warm up too much before road races and cool down too little afterward. Most of them start their races too quickly and finish too slowly, and most would feel better and do better by reversing those procedures.

The fastest races often seem the easiest. The slowest ones usually hurt the most.

The race doesn't end at the finish line. The most criticial part of the schedule is yet to come: the recovery portion. Spend at least one day recovering for each mile of racing.

The Running Life

Aging is a myth, or at least the supposed rate of decline in performance with age is. All runners have the potential to improve for many years, regardless of when they start to race.

Five to ten years is a common improvement period. That seems to be about as long as most people can tolerate serious training, especially when their times level off.

The "golden age of running" is a personal matter. You look back most fondly on the years when every course was new, every run offered a fresh revelation, every race a better time.

There is life after racing. Some of your best running days begin after the last PR is set and the pressure to perform eases off.

Pacing applies to a career, not just to individual runs and races. Pace each day as if it were a step, each year as if it were a mile in a marathon, and do nothing in any of the parts that might jeopardize the whole.

Running interests evolve through stages. In Stage One, you exercise to get fit; in Stage Two, you train to go farther and faster; in Stage Three, you run for its own sake.

THE RUNNING BODY

*F*or many of my early years, starting when I was ten, I delivered newspapers. This fixed several habits: getting up early, moving around outside right away, keeping up with the news, and looking out for dogs.

In my hometown, bad weather and newspaper rules precluded tossing papers onto lawns. Carriers had to place them inside screen doors, in boxes on porches, or under bricks to keep the papers from blowing away or getting soaked.

Almost everyone in town owned a dog—usually a big, protective one—and *leash* was a dirty word. Delivering the newspaper properly meant venturing into the heart of the dog's territory, and I learned to think of each dog as a vicious killer until it proved otherwise.

Most dogs displayed their better nature after an initial show of snarling and barking. Others put up token defenses before wandering away. Some slept through my morning visits once they realized that I was leaving something, not taking. Many of the dogs along the route came to treat me as a friend who would do what their masters wouldn't: take them for a morning stroll.

I was able to make friends with all the dogs except one named Woody. He always bared his yellowed teeth, flashed wide and murderous eyes, and raised the black fur on his back as I approached his house. In his youth, Woody had tangled with a car or a power tool, losing one of his front legs. He could still move faster on three legs than any paperboy could on two, and he practiced speedwork against me each morning.

Nature builds in spare parts to let animals lose some and go on living. But while this three-legged dog survived, he never lived fully again. He turned bitter and mean after the accident. It was as if he never forgave the human race for taking away one of his legs, and I was his first chance each morning to take revenge.

Any good life has four "legs" under it. Not physical legs with bones, muscles, tendons, cartilage, and joints, but real pegs which hold us up, keep us balanced and moving. These four supports are health, diet, activity, and peace.

- Health—the absence of crippling injury or illness. Good health isn't guaranteed just because we run. While running may give certain types of health tune-ups, it doesn't spell everlasting freedom from injury and illness. Running causes some problems and does nothing to prevent others.
- Diet—enough of the right kind of food to keep us moving; not so much that it leaves us sluggish. Runners can eat a little more than people who aren't active and still not gain weight. But running does not grant a license for gluttony.
- Activity—work and play that we do because we want to, not because we must. It feels good to work at playing. Everyone needs some absorbing activity that may seem hard and boring to an outsider, but which is really the closest an adult can come to child's play.
- Peace—the chance and the ability to relax; a sense of calm, humor, and contentment. Make friends with yourself. Heed the survival instincts signaling fatigue, pain, and tension. By working with them instead of against them, we can accomplish more with less stress.

Our fitness balances on these four legs. I talk about them as separate pegs, but they're really a delicate, interconnected system. When the whole system is fit, we don't notice its parts. It moves along with the coordination of a running animal. But let one part go awry, and the system falls out of synch.

Lameness in one of the legs seldom stops us cold. It does worse. It eats away at our joy of moving smoothly. Like the three-legged dog, we can exist without any one of these legs. I suppose we could even survive if all of them went lame. But the loss of good function anywhere would surely turn everything sour.

C H A P T E R   F O U R

The Work

Aerobic Effects

When you first became a runner, two dramatic changes took place inside. You trained the aerobic mechanism, and you adapted to the stresses. The combined effects opened the way to longer, faster, smoother running.

Running is—or should be—essentially aerobic. Kenneth Cooper, M.D., in his ground-breaking book *Aerobics,* defined this type of activity.

"These exercises demand oxygen without producing an intolerable oxygen debt [such as sprinting does], so that they can be continued for long periods. They activate the training effect and start producing all those wonderful changes in your body. Your lungs begin processing more air and with less effort. Your heart grows stronger, pumping more blood with fewer strokes, the blood supply to your muscles improves, and your total blood volume increases. In short, you are improving your body's capacity to bring in oxygen and deliver it to the tissue cells, where it is combined with foodstuffs to produce energy. You are increasing your oxygen consumption and, consequently, your endurance capacity."

You know you're running aerobically if you can pass the so-called "talk test." Try talking to a friend while running, or whistle if you're alone. If you can carry your end of the conversation or can mouth a tune, you're safely into the aerobic-exercise range.

The human body is an amazingly pliable instrument. It adapts to almost any activity it is given, balking only to protect itself from eventual destruction. The responses to physical activity are standard. Everyone reacts to exercise with the same general set of adjustments. Together, they're called the "training effect."

The sudden jumps in ability made by a new runner are measurable evidence of good changes happening inside. The resting pulse typically drops by ten or more beats a minute in the first few months of regular running. The oxygen-uptake reading, a measure of the lungs' ability take in and distribute this endurance fuel, improves by ten percent or more. The blood pressure typically decreases by a similar amount. These and other changes in your internal chemistry and physiology add up to the big improvements in performance rather quickly.

Dr. Cooper, who has analyzed the experiences of millions of beginning runners, writes: "I like to think of the training effect as preventive medicine. It builds a bulwark in the body against most of the common cripplers. . . . If you've started a little late, if one of the cripplers has already made its mark on you, the training effect can become curative medicine as well."

The first step a new runner must take is to clear away the effects of a sedentary life. Reduce the excess fat that has collected under the skin. Tone up the muscles. Inject more oxygen into the system. Strengthen and slow the heart. Correct degenerative problems if they haven't progressed too far.

Even when an individual starts from what the physiologists call the "deconditioned state," the changes are immediate and often dramatic. They follow Cooper's outline, and can be measured easily by keeping three types of records: (1) running performances in terms of distance and pace; (2) pulse—not only resting but also while exercising—and the rate of recovery; and (3) weight.

As training progresses, a runner should automatically go farther and faster with equal or even decreased effort. The heart pumps slower at rest, goes safely to a higher maximum, and returns to normal faster than before. Weight—if it was too high at the start—almost always drops, or at least "fat weight" is replaced by more useful and attractive "muscle weight."

These changes come with time, but they can't be rushed. They arrive only at their own pace. By trying to push it, the runner succeeds only in driving himself or herself *lower* on the fitness ladder. The same activity that builds up can also tear down if taken in improper doses.

This brings us again to the second key principle of running fitness: gradual adaptation to stress. What you want to do is vaccinate yourself against the distressing aspects of this exercise. A vaccine is a small, carefully controlled dose of medicine. Taken in proper amounts, it sets up an immunity to a disease, but when taken in excess the "cure" can be worse than the ailment.

In this case, aerobic unfitness is the "disease" and aerobic running the vaccine. You try to build an immunity to the stresses of running *by running*. When the doses are small and their increases carefully controlled, you grow stronger. But when the amounts are excessive, you overwhelm the system's ability to adapt and tear yourself down.

However, with patience and regular application of right amounts of stress, anyone can accomplish the two main goals of any fitness routine: increased immunity to fatigue, and faster, smoother movement.

Good and Bad Stress

The human body/mind is a symphony. Some of the individual instruments boom, some whisper. Together, they make melodies, harmonies, and rhythms. When the individual parts blend as intended, you don't hear individual parts. You hear the musical whole, and it's beautiful. But a single instrument out of tune can destroy the music and make you painfully aware of the discord.

Stresses are normal and natural parts of living. They come from many directions and in various combinations (see Table 4.1). We absorb them into the pace of life. They only become obvious and harmful when they come in too-heavy amounts for too long a period. Then off-key notes stand out. The signs and symptoms of overstressing are easy to spot (Chapter 5 covers them in detail). If detected early and analyzed correctly, they can be reduced before doing serious damage. But if overall stress loads remain high, they lead to illness, injury, or psychological collapse.

Table 4.1 *Stresses of Living*

The runner doesn't move through a vacuum. The act of running is only one of many stresses acting on a runner. At least seven families of stresses combine to produce a single result: the draining of adaptation reserves. The major stresses and examples of each follow.

1. *Work:* Specific stress of running, and general stresses of day's physical and mental labor

2. *Emotional:* Anxiety, depression, anger

3. *Social:* Isolation; overcrowding

4. *Dietary:* Too much food, too little, wrong type

5. *Rest:* Inadequate recovery from hard work; sleep deprivation

6. *Health:* Injury; illness; infection

7. *Environmental:* Heat and cold; high altitude and air pollution

---

Hans Selye, M.D., a Canadian medical researcher, has spent most of his life studying the stress phenomenon. He has written that every disease is a symptom of excessive stress, and that many of the physical and emotional breakdowns which are common in athletes come from this same source.

"When we finished our laborious analysis of its nature," writes Selye in his book *The Stress of Life,* "stress turned out to be something quite simple to understand. It is essentially the wear and tear in the body caused by life at any one time."

Selye says that a person exposed to this wear and tear erects defenses to counteract it. The body has a reservoir of "adaptive energy" for handling everyday battering, plus a reserve supply for emergencies. But if the doses of stress are too heavy and prolonged, the individual can't cope. The reserves are drained, and he or she goes into what Selye calls the "exhaustion phase of the General Adaptation Syndrome."

This is when the discordant notes surface: sudden drop in performance, drastic weight change, rapid pulse, disturbed sleep, carryover fatigue from one day to the next, colds or fever, anxiety or irritability, pain.

According to Selye, adaptation energy resembles a special kind of bank account which we can use by making withdrawals but cannot increase by deposits. He says we only replenish part of what we squander. "When superficial adaptation energy is exhausted through exertion, it can slowly be restored from a deeper store during rest. This gives a certain plasticity to our resistance. It also protects us from wasting adaptation energy too lavishly in certain foolish moments, because acute fatigue automatically stops us."

But he warns that each time a person ignores stress symptoms and digs deeper into the "frozen assets," he or she risks permanent injury.

Experiments on animals have clearly shown that each exposure [to excess stress] leaves an indelible scar, in that it uses up reserves of adaptability which cannot be replaced. It is the restoration of superficial adaptation energy that tricks us into believing that the loss has been made good. Actually it has only been covered from reserves—at the cost of depleting reserves.

"We can compare this feeling of having suffered no loss to the careless optimism of a spendthrift who keeps forgetting that whenever he restores the vanishing supply of dollars in his wallet by withdrawing from the invisible stocks of his bank account, the loss has not really been made good. There was merely a transfer of money from a less accessible to a more accessible form.

Okay. So how does all this theory translate into practical terms for a runner? Avoid stress? Not at all. If you're going to improve your running, it is essential to court a specific type of stress and to travel a thin line between enough and too much.

One solution might be to think of yourself as a violin string. Like the string, you have a great creative capacity. But that potential is wasted when you lie limp and unused. Only when you're stretched are you filling your intended role. But the stretching can go too far. When pressures pull too hard in opposite directions, *snap!*

The trick is to find a point of stretch, a level of activity, that makes music while holding resiliency in reserve. When emergencies come up—either real or artificial, in the form of hard training and racing—you should be able to meet them by stretching more instead of snapping.

Hans Selye concludes, "The goal is certainly not to avoid stress. Stress is a part of life. It is a natural by-product of all-out activities. There is no more justification for avoiding stress than for shunning food, exercise or love. But in order to express yourself fully, you must first find your optimum stress level, and then use your adaptation energy at a rate and in a direction adjusted to the innate structure of your body and mind. It is not easy. It takes much practice and constant self-analysis."

The Medicine

Self-Inflicted Suffering

This is not a pleasant subject, but it's one that every runner must eventually face. What happens when you can't run?

Unfortunately, running is not a perfectly safe activity. It is work, and it can easily cross the line into *overwork*. As more runners look for the thrill of victory, more experience the agony of defeat—the worst loss being inactivity from stress-induced injury and illness.

The injury rate from this seemingly non-violent sport is alarming. In any year, one runner in two is hurt badly enough to require a layoff, medical treatment, or both. Most of these injuries are self-inflicted. They result neither from a competitor's deliberate blows, as might happen in football, nor from random accidents such as hitting a rock while skiing. The stresses of running itself are responsible in nearly all cases.

Certain viruses such as the common cold and the flu take hold for the same reasons. You're constantly exposed to these diseases, yet they only surface after stress has broken down the body's natural defenses. At least ninety percent of running injuries and illnesses grow out of what the sports doctors call "overuse": too much wear and tear on a body not conditioned to handle this stress.

Table 5.1 *Warning Signs*

When the stress load becomes too heavy, for whatever reason, certain mild symptoms appear. These warn that more serious trouble might develop if preventive action isn't taken. Prevention usually involves reducing or eliminating one or more of the stresses listed in Table 4.1. The most telling signs of impending injury or illness, adapted from a list originally compiled by Tom Osler in his classic booklet, *The Conditioning of Distance Runners,* follow.

1. Resting pulse rate significantly higher than normal when taken first thing in the morning.

2. Difficulty falling asleep and staying asleep.

3. Sores in and around the mouth, and other skin eruptions in non-adolescents.

4. Any symptom of a cold or the flu—sniffles, sore throat, or fever.

5. Swollen, tender glands in the neck, groin, or underarms.

6. Labored breathing during the mild exertion of daily running.

7. Dizziness or nausea before, during, or after running.

8. Clumsiness—for instance, tripping or kicking oneself during a run over rather smooth ground.

9. Any muscle or tendon pain or stiffness that remains after the first few minutes of a run.

10. No feeling of anticipation before running, and no feeling of accomplishment afterward; dread and depression are the dominant emotions.

In this last fact lies hope. Because you cause most of your own running ailments, you also have the power to prevent them. The damage doesn't often happen randomly, without cause or reason. Athletic ailments aren't punishment from the wrathful gods, but are predictable results of too much work and too little attention to obvious warnings. You alone decide if you will be a victim of pain or a victor over it.

Runners' Injuries

A running injury doesn't usually strike with sudden and devastating consequences, like a compound fracture of the leg. These problems are more in the nature of slow, steady erosion that wears down the body.

The physical pain of most running injuries doesn't even amount to much, hurting less than an average headache or toothache, if at all, when you are at rest. However, a sore spot the size of a dime can be debilitating when you put your full weight on it.

Surveys in running magazines indicate the following.

- The weakest link in runners is the knee. About one in five injured runners has a knee problem.
- Nearly as many break down at the Achilles tendon, the thin band of tissue connecting the heel bone with the calf muscles.
- Ten percent suffer "shin splints"—an imprecise term covering ailments in the front of the lower leg. These range from tendinitis to stress fractures.
- Forefoot strains and stress fractures, severe heel pain, and damage to the arch account for at least seven percent of injuries.

There isn't space here to diagnose and treat each injury. Better that we talk about why they happen, in hopes of reducing the high toll. Injuries occur for four main reasons.

1. Overwork—too much work for the muscles and limbs to handle, causing the weakest link to break.
2. Faulty equipment—usually meaning shoes which either are inadequate for the purpose or are worn out. (See Chapter 10 for a discussion of shoe selection.)
3. Weakness and inflexibility—muscles which are so overspecialized that the slightest unusual twist strains them. (See Chapter 15 for advice on supplemental exercises.)
4. Mechanical problems—either faults in the running form or in the way the foot meets the ground. (See Chapter 14 for material on form.)

While treating the symptoms of injury (see Table 5.2), you should also do some detective work into causes. Look to sensible workloads, well-made and well-cared-for shoes, supplemental strength-stretch exercises and mechanical improvements for permanent cures.

Runners' Illnesses

Running makes some people ill—literally. But it can also act as preventive medicine or an aid to treatment. It all depends on how you use it or abuse it.

The good news first. Evidence gleaned from several scientific studies indicates that runners as a group suffer fewer colds than non-runners. This apparently has to do with normally increased body heat which may destroy some of the "bugs." Runners also note that the congestion of a cold clears up more quickly if they run in its waning stages.

Table 5.2 *Recovery Road*

An injury has knocked you off your feet. What to do now? Whatever the problem is, the road back to health follows a similar path. It allows you to heal and still stay somewhat active—to satisfy the need of regular activity without aggravating the problem. Choose your proper effort level, then exercise at the normal time and for the normal period of time. If you can't run steadily without limping, mix walking and running; if all running is impossible, just walk; if walking hurts too much, bike or swim.

1. *Biking or swimming.* These activities take nearly all the pressure off most injuries, while still giving steady workouts. They make you feel you still have some control over yourself.

2. *Walking.* Start it as soon as you can move around favoring the injured limb. Continue as long as pain doesn't become intolerable. (These limitations apply at all stages.)

3. *Walking mixed with running.* As the walks become too easy, add intervals of slow running: as little as one minute in five at first, then gradually building up the amounts of running until reaching. . . .

4. *Running mixed with walking.* The balance tips in favor of the runs, but you keep inserting brief walks at this stage when steady pressure can't yet be tolerated.

5. *Running again.* Approach it cautiously for a while: a little slower than normal and with no long or fast tests until the typical daily runs can be handled comfortably.

A similar plan, minus stage one, can be followed as you cautiously return to the road after illnesses.

However, continued hard running in the face of early symptoms can turn a mild cold into a dreadful one, and may lead to side-effects such as bronchitis. Catching cold means you already have worked too hard. Don't compound the problem.

George Sheehan, M.D., as medical columnist for a running magazine, spends a large part of each day advising ailing runners. A summary of his advice for treating common illnesses is presented here.

- *Colds*—"I treat them with respect. It is my feeling that they represent a breakdown of the defense system. The cold is an early warning symptom of exhaustion." Dr. Sheehan advises that you heed your body's warnings and cut back or even cut out training for the first one to three days of the cold, "then resume at a slow pace for relatively short distances. However, do not wait until all symptoms subside." Start running then to clear away the cold's debris.

- *Fever*—most commonly associated with the flu. "Don't run with a fever!" warns Dr. Sheehan. "After that, as a rule of thumb, take two days easy for each day of fever. A week of fever and symptoms, therefore, would need an additional two weeks' recovery period. Exhausting runs should be avoided at this time, or recurrence is a distinct possibility."

Sheehan adds, "When you come back, it is difficult to know whether fatigue is physical or psychological. There is, however, a simple test for this. Start your runs very slowly until you start to sweat. This usually takes about six minutes. At this point, you should feel like running—no matter how you felt at the beginning. If you don't, and five more minutes confirms it, pack it in."

Exhaustion is the common denominator in these illnesses, and avoiding it is the best medicine.

Preventive Medicine

Hans Selye, M.D., was never a serious runner, yet the Canadian physiologist provides a basis for modern training with his General Adaptation Syndrome (GAS) theory, detailed in Chapter 4.

To review, Selye's theory argues that a person exposed to stress (running is one stress among many) erects defenses to counteract it. If the stress is applied in small, regular doses, the body adapts to it by growing stronger; but if the doses are too heavy, the body can't cope. It goes into the exhaustion phase of the syndrome, becoming highly susceptible to physical breakdowns.

The trick in running training, then, is to run enough to build and not so much that you tear down. This same exercise can be either helpful or hurtful, depending on how you decide to apply it. How do you determine the right amount?

Adaptive success and failure are easy to detect. Improved performance accompanied by pain-free running mean you're adapting nicely to this stress. On the other hand, as you approach the exhausted state, your body and mind send out danger signals. These include persistent soreness and stiffness, nervousness, unexplained drops in performance, and many other symptoms (summarized in Table 5.1).

A number of signals tell us when we're in and out of tune. It's a wise runner who develops a sensitive "eye" to the body's signals. By reading and interpreting these signs, he or she can go a long way toward stopping trouble at its source.

C H A P T E R   S I X

The
Diet

Eating and Drinking

You are what you eat—but as a runner you also very often are what you *don't* eat. That last remark carries immediate and long-term implications.

Eating too much of the wrong items too soon before you run has uncomfortable consequences, ranging from cramps to nausea to vomiting. The old admonition not to swim for at least an hour after eating also applies to running.

The long-term result of overeating is, of course, excessive weight—or, more specifically, excessive *fat*. Most of us carry too much of it. Even the so-called "normal" weights listed on insurance-company charts may be too high for a runner seeking improved performances. Each additional pound above your ideal weight has a direct, negative influence on your running, since you must lift that burden 1500 times each mile. Regular running tends to reduce weight, but not by dramatic amounts. Only running *plus* dieting can accomplish that.

Drinking is a special concern. Runners, says the exercise physiologist who has studied them most extensively, often become "chronically dehydrated." David Costill, Ph.D., of Ball State University has found that high-mileage athletes dehydrate day after day and may never make up the losses if they rely on thirst alone to tell them when to drink. *Sudden* drops in weight aren't signs of health, but are signals of fluid deficits.

Certain types of food intake do offer hope for eventual improvement in performances. But you should be careful not to rely too heavily on this hope because food and drink aren't ends but beginnings. Good nutrition is a catalyst which allows running to take place, but it offers no substitute for work and no shortcut to success. No runner ever ate and drank his or her way to success.

Vitamin and mineral supplements? The final verdict isn't in yet on the results of heavy supplementation, and experts still argue over the value or worthlessness of extra vitamins and minerals for runners. You can answer that question for yourself after reading what nutritional experts say elsewhere.

I also won't rehash the essentials of a balanced diet here. Similar rules apply to everyone, runner or not, and this is a subject for another book.

What Not to Eat

It's said you don't appreciate the water until the well runs dry. And you don't appreciate how important nutrition is until something goes wrong inside. If you're eating correctly, you ignore your internal organs. But when they scream for relief, you must pay attention.

Runners operate under physical and sometimes emotional stress and strain. This temporarily stressful situation makes runners peculiarly susceptible to diet-related irregularities that don't often strike people who operate on a lower plane.

There are two main causes of internal distress.

- *Eating too much, too soon before running.* We run best on an empty or nearly empty stomach. Arthur Lydiard, the prominent coach from New Zealand, observes that runners rarely "collapse from malnutrition" during a run. But they do have problems of the opposite type: doubling over with side pains called "stitches," making "pitstops" along the way (few runners ever complain about irregularity), or simply carrying an unpleasant sloshing and bloated feeling. Eat lightly, if at all, in the last hours before running. Your body holds abundant stored energy to carry you through.
- *Eating the wrong foods at the wrong times.* Certain people can't tolerate certain food groups, and they react violently to them—particularly in times of stress. Surprisingly, two chief culprits may be the "perfect food" and the "staff of life." George Sheehan, M.D., the sport's most prominent medical advisor, points out that a great number of pleas for help come from runners who don't tolerate milk and bread products very well. Dr. Sheehan identifies other suspect foods as the highly allergenic ones (chocolate, shellfish, etc.) and excessive roughage (raw fruits and vegetables, whole grains). Even if you don't have a specific intolerance, you're wise to avoid most or all of these items—along with anything heavy in fat, which digests slowly—in the last meal before a run.

The one basic rule in these two areas: Err on the side of too little rather than too much; when in doubt, *don't*.

Weight Watching

Nutritional advisors tell you to find your proper weight and then maintain it. But arriving at the ideal figure—either pinpointing it or achieving it—isn't as easy as they make it sound.

One method is to labor through a trial-and-error process, measuring weight against performance. This can take years. Another way is to consult a standard weight chart. This almost invariably lets you weigh too much.

Another—the best way—is to measure your body-fat percentage. This is the most accurate measure of ideal body composition ("ideals" generally are listed as twelve to fifteen percent for men, and eighteen to twenty-two percent for women), but it is a technique not readily available to most of us. So we're left with rough rules of thumb which don't take into account the vast differences in frame sizes. These apply to people of average build. One such estimate comes from Irwin Maxwell Stillman, M.D., author of a number of diet books.

In his formula, men start from a base of 110 pounds, then add five and one-half pounds for every inch of height above five feet. A man six feet tall, for instance, adds sixty-six pounds for a target weight of 176 pounds.

Women start from 100 pounds (not 110) under the Stillman formula. They add five pounds (not five and one-half) for each inch over five feet. A five-foot-five woman, then, is allowed 125 pounds.

Dr. Stillman adds, "If you're an athlete, it's best to weigh about five pounds less than the ideal weight listed."

Running does burn calories, but not as quickly as you might suspect. The figure generally quoted is 100 per mile (Table 6.1 provides more exact estimates). At that rate, you must run ten miles or more to get rid of that milk shake you drank last night. You must run thirty-five miles to drop a single pound, and that is assuming you eat nothing new in the meantime.

If you plan to lose weight by running, you must accept the fact that you'll take it off gradually. Say you're running five miles, seven days a week, while keeping your intake constant. That effort equals about 3500 calories a week, so you can plan on losing a pound every week. In a little more than three months, this adds up to a significant ten pounds. With dietary limitations, the timetable may be speeded up.

But again a warning: Resist the temptation to indulge in quick-loss schemes. These usually involve artificial water-weight drops along with declines in energy. The first thing you cut out while dieting is high-carbohydrate foods from the grains, potatoes, and sugars—the very items you need to sustain running. Excessive sweating from running in heavy clothing may take off several pounds, but this loss doesn't stay lost.

Think of weight reduction as a long-term project which will be permanent on completion.

Table 6.1 *Caloric Cost of Running*

Calories Burned Per Mile

Multiply your number of miles times the caloric cost per mile for your pace and weight. A net expenditure (amount burned minus amount eaten) of about 3500 calories equals a one-pound weight loss.

Weight (pounds)	6:00	7:00	Pace per Mile 8:00	9:00	10:00
100	70	68	66	64	63
110	77	75	73	70	69
120	83	81	79	77	76
130	90	87	85	83	82
140	97	94	92	90	88
150	103	100	98	96	94
160	110	107	104	102	100
170	117	112	111	107	106
180	123	120	117	114	112
190	130	126	123	120	118
200	137	133	129	126	124

Calories Burned Per Minute

Multiply your number of minutes times the caloric cost per minute for your pace and weight.

Weight (pounds)	6:00	7:00	Pace per Mile 8:00	9:00	10:00
100	12	11	9	8	7
110	13	12	10	8	7
120	14	12	10	9	8
130	15	13	11	9	8

Table 6.1—*Continued*

Weight (pounds)	6:00	7:00	Pace per Mile 8:00	9:00	10:00
140	16	14	12	10	9
150	17	14	12	10	9
160	18	15	13	11	10
170	19	16	14	12	11
180	20	17	15	13	11
190	21	18	16	14	12
200	22	19	16	14	12

The tables are adapted from statistics compiled by Drs. Bruce C. Harper, James D. Miller, and James C. Thompson. (*Journal of the American Medical Association,* April 1974.)

Drinks for the Road

While fluid losses are temporary, they're still vitally important to runners. The significant effects are negative ones, ranging from impaired performance to heat collapse.

Here, in simplest terms, is what happens. A pint of sweat weighs about a pound, and a runner can lose a quart before noticing anything is wrong. As the deficit grows, the body temperature rises proportionately, pushing toward a critical level.

C. H. Wyndham, a South African, has done extensive research on heat responses. He says, "Up to a water deficit of about three percent, body temperature varies between about 101 and 102 degrees. But with an increase in water deficit above three percent, rectal temperatures increased in proportion to the extent of water deficit."

The two- or three-degree rise is normal and acceptable for a runner. But increases beyond that point bear watching. American physiologist David Costill has measured sweat losses as great as ten percent in marathon runners and temperatures as high as 105 degrees. Body heat only slightly higher than that can lead to heat exhaustion or heat stroke, the latter being potentially fatal. (Don't be alarmed here. You're unlikely to overheat during your comfortably paced daily runs lasting less than an hour.)

Drinking immediately before, during, and after runs won't completely eliminate losses. But it can replace enough of the lost fluid and cool the temperatures to a degree where exercise is at least safe.

Table 6.2 *Three-Percent Sweat Debt*

Fluid losses exceeding three percent of body weight represent significant dehydration. This table translates the three-percent figure into pounds for runners of various sizes. Pre- and post-run weight checks are advisable in hot, humid weather. To get the most accurate reading of your sweat debt, weigh yourself right after the run—before drinking.

Pre-Run	Post-Run
100 pounds	97 pounds
105 pounds	102 pounds
110 pounds	107 pounds
115 pounds	112 pounds
120 pounds	116 pounds
125 pounds	121 pounds
130 pounds	126 pounds
135 pounds	131 pounds
140 pounds	136 pounds
145 pounds	141 pounds
150 pounds	145 pounds
155 pounds	150 pounds
160 pounds	155 pounds
165 pounds	160 pounds
170 pounds	165 pounds
175 pounds	170 pounds
180 pounds	175 pounds
185 pounds	180 pounds
190 pounds	184 pounds
195 pounds	189 pounds
200 pounds	194 pounds

Dr. Costill says runners tend to let the sensation of thirst set their drinking habits, and thirst sometimes fibs about true fluid needs. "In laboratory tests that required about eight pounds of sweat loss," says Costill, "we found that thirst was temporarily satisfied by drinking as little as one pound of water." (Water accounts for nearly all of the loss, and is the replacement drink of choice because it is absorbed quickly and with few or no complications.)

After a sweat loss that large, it may take several days to redress the balance. Chronic dehydration may result from repeated heavy drains and inadequate replacement. The best way to guard against this is to check your weight each day. If your down more than two pounds from the day before, you're a quart low on liquids. Drink up!

THE RUNNING ENVIRONMENT

*T*his is not a perfect world. You can't always run at the ideal time of day. The courses you run aren't often perfectly smooth and flat. The weather seldom is just right.

Rather than complain about these natural conditions—or worse, refuse to run when they aren't perfect—a runner must learn to adapt to the nature of things instead of expecting them to satisfy him or her. Learn ways of meeting and beating the forces which keep many runners from running as far or as often as they should. After all, only about one day a week is perfectly conducive to running, and that single day does not a runner make.

Take winter weather as an example. I learned early to accept winters as inevitable and to appreciate the value of cold-weather running. I came to view it not as a period to be suffered through, or as a time to be waited out indoors, or as a season to give up the sport in favor of one more suited to the snow and cold. I looked forward to winter running as a time to sneak ahead of runners who were hibernating until spring.

I took my first runs in Iowa, where it was thought in the 1950s that the only sane thing for an athlete to do between November and March was to stay in the gym, shooting baskets. I didn't leave the court voluntarily; I had to be forced outside.

The saddest—and luckiest—day of my young life came when the basketball coach gently told me there would be no place on his team for a five-foot-five, nearsighted guard. Earlier that year, I had discovered that football had no room for a timid 130-pound linebacker. The school had no baseball team. Track was my last chance to salvage athletic success.

I decided to jump the gun on the track season by running all winter, starting indoors because I still believed the rumor that my lungs would turn to popsicles if I breathed too much cold air.

"If it's okay with you," I said to the basketball coach," I'll just run around the gym floor."

He caught a loose ball, passed it back across the floor, then said, "I suppose it's okay, as long as you don't get in anybody's way. Just don't run here during ball practice."

Practice ended at six o'clock, and I couldn't wait that long to run. So I planned to squeeze in ten hard minutes before the players took over the court. The first day, I worked the tight turns like a Grand Prix driver. The next day, I limped into the gym on blistered feet and stiff ankles.

The coach noticed my pained walk. "What's wrong?" he asked. "Not ready to run yet?"

His words stung me. I forgot my soreness, went into the locker room, laced up my high-topped canvas shoes, tied my floppy gray sweatpants just below my chest, slipped into a hooded sweatshirt that hung to my thighs, added a stocking cap and gloves, and went outside to stay.

Winter running made me the runner I am now. That was not determined by what happened on the mild, sunny days of spring and autumn. Anyone can be a fair-weather runner. My attachment to the sport was tested and hardened on the so-called "bad days" when the crowds outside had disappeared.

The advice I would give—and take—about winter running applies to all environmental inconveniences: *Stay flexible*. Accept what you can't change, and change what you can't accept. Accept that you can't run as far or as fast as usual on some days. Change the time and place of running to make the most of the conditions you're given. More often than not, you can run something—and anything is better than nothing.

The
Logistics

When to Run?

"But I'm too busy. I don't have any time to run." Everyone is busy enough to fall back on that excuse for not running. No one has the time if he or she doesn't want to *make* the time. If you want to run, you *find* the time and stick to that time.

Morning, noon, or night, the effects are about the same. When you run depends upon the time of day when you operate best and when it's easiest for you to make time available for running.

We're all busy. No one can give you the time to run except yourself. Carve a chunk out of your day and protect it jealously. Set aside a half-hour to an hour for yourself, and don't give it up easily or often.

Some runners favor the first-thing-each-morning routine. It offers several advantages: (1) seldom do other people and activities interfere at that time of day; (2) you wake up quicker by literally getting your day off to a running start; (3) traffic is lightest at this hour; (4) the air is coolest and cleanest. The morning also has its down side: (1) the temptation to sleep through this time after a late night is great; (2) you're sorest and stiffest at this hour, and possibly most prone to injuries; (3) it's dark and cold for a large part of the year.

Those who run in the evening or at night prefer it for these reasons: (1) they feel loosest and most awake then; (2) it relieves the day's frustrations; (3) they like to run with other people, and it's easiest to find partners then. The minuses of running late: (1) work, family, and social obligations are most likely to eat into this time; (2) winter nights grow dark and cold early; (3) it's hard to delay dinner when you come home hungry and still have a run to take.

Noontime running is growing in popularity because it avoids some of the negatives of both morning and evening: no darkness, no sleepiness or stiffness, nothing else to do then except eat. Workers on a set schedule, with an hour off for lunch, find the time is better spent running than eating. The run blunts the appetite, gives a physical break from mental fatigue, and helps keep them alert all afternoon. The problems with noontime runs are: (1) finding a convenient place to run within close range of congested business or industrial areas; (2) finding a place to change clothes before the run and shower afterward; (3) feeling rushed to get in a long enough run within the available time.

These problems are being solved in areas where YMCAs, colleges, and parks and recreation departments open their facilities to runners at noon. Some progressive companies even provide showers to encourage employee exercise.

If you have such a changing room and really want to save time, do as Senator William Proxmire does. For years, he has commuted on foot from his home in Washington to Capitol Hill.

"I work it into my schedule so that it takes far less time than if I went out and set aside a certain time to run," says Proxmire. "I run to work. Of course, I'd have to come to work, anyway, and if I go by car during rush hour it would probably take me twenty-five minutes. I run that distance in thirty-five minutes. So the only cost is a thirty-five-minute, good, hard aerobic workout. Then at night I run-walk home. I have to go home, too, so it works out very nicely."

Proxmire says if you don't live within running range of work, "park on the outskirts [of town] and just get out and run the remaining two, three, four, or five miles, whatever you want to run. You can fit it into your day that way."

Where to Run?

"But I don't have any place to run." That's the second most common complaint from beginners. Look around you.

"Running country is everywhere," says coach Bill Bowerman. "Open your door, and you're in business. Run right out the door, run in a schoolyard, on a city street, at the beach, on a country road, or in a vacant lot. Run down a bicycle path, on a school track, around a golf course, through a park, in your backyard, in a gymnasium, in a supermarket parking lot. Anywhere."

Anywhere you can safely walk is suitable for running. But some places are better than others. If you have a choice, look for running areas which meet as many of the following criteria as possible:

1. Convenient enough that you don't have to drive to the start and back after finishing most runs. But don't become so wedded to the home courses that you avoid exploring other territory.
2. Relatively free of auto and pedestrian traffic. This cuts down on risk, air pollution, and self-consciousness.
3. Controlled dog population. Nothing ruins a run faster than an unleashed dog nipping at your heels.
4. Protection from wind and sun. Large trees along any route are a plus.
5. Pleasant sights and sounds. Nice views and silence don't make you a better runner, but they do make your runs better.

You may not have what seems to be an ideal place to run, like a path laid out specifically for running, as is the case in Bill Bowerman's hometown of Eugene, Oregon. But there are always plenty of places—the neighborhood streets, if nothing else is handy.

Choose a variety of routes for a variety of reasons and seasons. This is a good way to explore your surrounding area, for one thing. Also, you soon grow tired of a single path. Then, too, many of the best courses—the ones on softer ground—become impossible in rainy or snowy weather, and you need alternates.

Each of the four ways to lay out courses (see Figure 7.1) has advantages and limitations.

- *Point-to-point*. Starting and finishing at widely separated places. These routes are most pleasant to run because they involve no repeating, no circling back. They give a feeling of "getting somewhere." But that leaves you with the problem of getting back again.
- *Out-and-back*. Running to a turn-around point and then retracing your steps. These courses are the easiest to follow when you aren't quite sure where you are. But some runners don't like to repeat themselves.
- *Laps*. Going around and around the same circuit. This is a good way to run if you like to monitor your pace along the way; not so good if you get bored easily.
- *Loop*. Running one big circuit that starts and finishes in the same place, but never covers the same ground twice. It may be hard to follow, but it's the best way to run from the combined standpoints of convenience and enjoyment.

If you're interested in timing yourself, measure the routes. Accuracy of measurement depends on the method used. The easiest way to check distance is with a car; it is also the least accurate. Be warned that odometer measurements almost always produce slightly short measurements. That's because you can't cut corners as tightly when you drive as when you run. The correction factor is at least fifty yards per mile. Don't put much faith in the accuracy of times you run on courses measured this way.

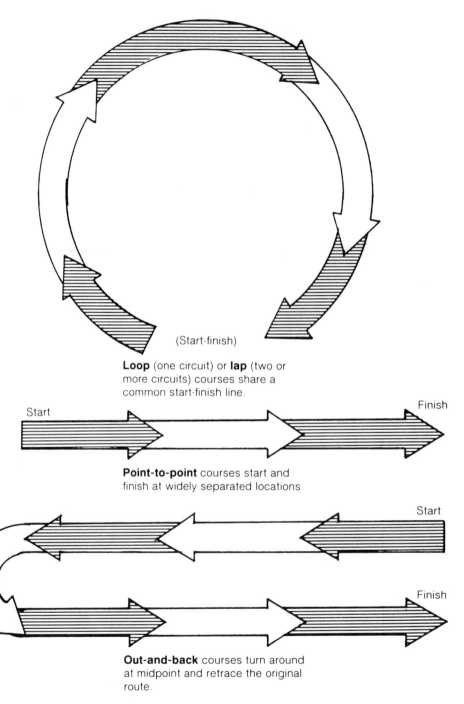

(Start-finish)

Loop (one circuit) or **lap** (two or more circuits) courses share a common start-finish line.

Point-to-point courses start and finish at widely separated locations

Out-and-back courses turn around at midpoint and retrace the original route.

Figure 7.1 Course Designs

If you want more precision, use a bicycle revolution counter. This device fits onto the front wheel of a bike. After it is calibrated against a precisely measured distance (such as a track), you can ride any route and find its distance within a yard per mile.

Such precision borders on hair-splitting. The concern with distances may be unnecessary, and you may not even need to worry about staying on fixed courses if you take an increasingly popular approach to measurement: running by time.

Forget about how *far* you run. Count minutes, not miles. Think only about how long you spend running. Start your digital stopwatch at the beginning, shut it off at the finish, and record the time period rather than the distance.

This approach offers several benefits. The switch to running with time relieves the pressure of trying to run a distance *against* time. The natural tendency when running a distance is to finish it as quickly as possible, pushing yourself too hard in the process. However, you can't make a period of time pass any faster. In fact, it seems to take longer when you try to rush it. So the tendency is to run the time at a comfortable pace.

The more immediate practical advantage of running by time is freedom. You're free from designing and measuring courses, free from following those routes step by step, free to alter old paths and explore new ones while filling the time quota.

What to Do, When?

Tom Osler is one of the brightest thinkers in running, even though his name doesn't normally appear on the sport's "guru" lists. His *Conditioning of Distance Runners,* published in 1966, was one of the first great advice books. Neither that nor his *Serious Runner's Handbook* ever reached the audiences they deserved, so Osler remains one of the unsung geniuses of the sport.

One of Osler's hidden gems deals with seasonal ups and downs. They are as normal and natural as the shifts from summer to fall, winter to spring, he says.

"One can rarely maintain a high performance level for more than three months," Osler tells long-distance competitors. "Heavy racing must therefore be terminated after about three months or when symptoms of energy depletion [see Table 5.1] are first observed."

Osler found during his own racing career that his years fell neatly into two cycles lasting about six months apiece. Each cycle held a "high" period of about three months and a "low" of the same length. He raced best and stayed healthiest if he emphasized his racing and race-like training at the high times and avoided it during the lows. The highs tended to come in spring and fall, the lows in winter and summer.

Those periods match the traditional seasons of the sport. Before year-round road racing grew up in the United States, before there were summer all-comers track meets, we ran track from about March to May and cross-country from September to November. We ran easily, if at all, between racing seasons.

No one would want a return to those bad old days. The *chance* to race year-round is a wonderful advance. But it puts the responsibility on us to *choose* when we'll race and when we won't. The opportunities have improved, but the rules haven't changed. It's still a very rare runner who can race well indefinitely.

Arthur Lydiard, the best-known coach of the past twenty-five years, says, "You can't race well year-round, because your condition will only take you so far." He warns that when you're racing hard, you deplete yourself. Eventually "you're going to have to go back and start to build up again."

It makes good sense to match highs and lows to the seasons of the year. The best weather and most of the best races come in spring and fall, and the least attractive racing occurs in the cold and hot months. Schedule your year to take advantage of the calendar's natural ups and downs.

In the timeless words of Ecclesiastes, everything has its season: ". . . a time to sow and a time to reap, a time to break down and a time to build up."

The Conditions

The Sky

As a runner, you don't need a weatherman to know which way the wind blows. You live with the elements. If you live anywhere but on the western and southern fringes of the United States, you taste the extremes of heat and cold.

An important fact to recognize when dealing with these elements is the difference between standing outside in the heat or cold, and running under these same conditions. Heat is worse for a runner than it might seem at the start, and cold isn't so bad. Wind and altitude offer mixed results.

Heat. A run on a hot day greatly increases the body's heat production, so a nice afternoon for suntanning beside the pool may be a disastrous one for running. As internal heat goes up, the body compensates by sweating. Sweat has to be replaced with water and other chemicals.

As noted in Chapter 6, if more than three percent of the weight is lost by sweating, performance is affected. If more than twice that much drains away, health itself is threatened. Remember to check the percentage by weighing yourself before and after hot-weather runs. Drink before and after running, and even during.

Heat-Safety Index

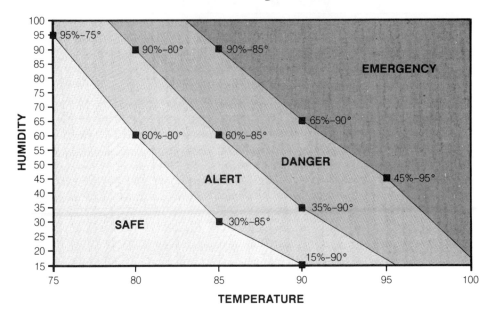

Figure 8.1 Heat-Safety Index. "Safe" temperature-humidity readings generally allow for normal activity, "alert" conditions require caution during long, hard runs, and "danger" levels may demand a reduction of training. Strenuous running is not recommended during "emergency" conditions. Source: *Jog, Run, Race* by Joe Henderson. Copyright © 1977 Joe Henderson. Reprinted by permission.

Also consider the humidity reading, which can make hot days feel even hotter. The closer the air is to the saturation point, the slower your sweat evaporates and the less well the air cools you. (Figure 8.1 lists combined heat/humidity factors and their effects.)

Cold. The body's heating mechanism that makes you miserable on hot days can make running more pleasant on cold ones. At all but the extremes of cold and wind, you warm up and stay comfortable if you're dressed well.

On typical winter days, there is little danger of frostbite if you keep moving and have your hands and ears covered. There is even less danger of "freezing the lungs" from breathing icy air. If the air had that much-feared effect, it would freeze your mouth and throat long before it reached the lungs.

Humidity makes summer weather unbearable. In winter, it's the wind. Temperatures feel colder than the thermometer shows on windy days. Each mile per hour of wind drops the apparent temperature by about one degree. Wind-chills below minus-twenty degrees carry "increased danger" of frostbite, according to Figure 8.2, and those below minus-seventy pose "great danger."

The proper clothing helps neutralize the extremes of weather. Figure 8.3 pictures the sensibly dressed runner. (For more on this subject, see Chapter 10.)

Wind-Chill Readings

Temperature (Fahrenheit)

	40	35	30	25	20	15	10	5	0	−5	−10	−15	−20	−25	−30	−35	−40	−45	−50	−55	−60
											Equivalent Chill Temperature										
Calm	40	35	30	25	20	15	10	5	0	−5	−10	−15	−20	−25	−30	−35	−40	−45	−50	−55	−60
5	35	30	25	20	15	10	5	0	−5	−10	−15	−20	−25	−30	−35	−40	−45	−50	−55	−65	−70
10	30	20	15	10	5	0	−10	−15	−20	−25	−35	−40	−45	−50	−60	−65	−70	−75	−80	−90	−95
15	25	15	10	0	−5	−10	−20	−25	−30	−40	−45	−50	−60	−65	−70	−80	−85	−90	−100	−105	−110
20	20	10	5	0	−10	−15	−25	−30	−35	−45	−50	−60	−65	−75	−80	−85	−95	−100	−110	−115	−120
25	15	10	0	−5	−15	−20	−30	−35	−45	−50	−60	−65	−75	−80	−90	−95	−105	−110	−120	−125	−135
30	10	5	0	−10	−20	−25	−30	−40	−50	−55	−65	−70	−80	−85	−95	−100	−105	−115	−120	−130	−140
35	10	5	−5	−10	−20	−25	−35	−40	−50	−60	−65	−70	−80	−90	−100	−105	−115	−120	−130	−135	−145
40*	10	0	−5	−15	−20	−30	−35	−45	−55	−60	−70	−75	−85	−95	−100	−110	−115	−125	−130	−140	−150

—Little Danger

Increasing Danger
(Flesh may freeze
within one minute)

Great Danger
(Flesh may freeze
within 30 seconds)

*Winds above 40 m.p.h. have little additional effect.

Figure 8.2 Wind-Chill Readings. Source: *Jog, Run, Race* by Joe Henderson. Copyright © 1977 Joe Henderson. Reprinted by permission.

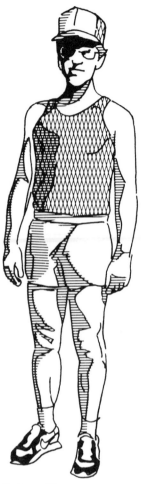 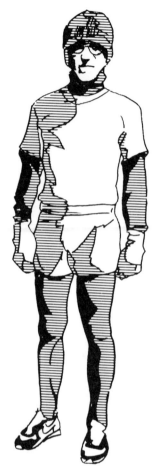 

Hot weather
Dress in minimal light-colored clothing (such as mesh baseball style cap, mesh top) that both protects from the sun and "breathes."

Cold weather
Dress in several layers of clothing, for instance, tights and turtleneck shirt under shorts and T-shirt; and gloves and stocking cap to protect head and hands.

Wet, cool weather
Dress in light, rain-repellent clothing. Wear baseball style cap to keep rain out of face. Gloves are optional.

Figure 8.3 Clothes for All Seasons

Wind. Nature isn't always fair. If half of your run is into the wind, the other half with it, and the wind speed is constant, you'll spend more effort bucking the wind than you'll save with it at your back. The difference is significant, and should be taken into account on windy days.

Choose courses that take maximum advantage of tailwinds, while reducing the energy lost to headwinds. This is particularly critical in winter, when the chilling effect compounds the typical energy drain of facing a wind. If you must run an out-and-back course on a cold and windy day, take the "out" portion into the wind, and return with it behind you so you'll stay warmer. In hot weather, you might want to reverse that procedure to take advantage of the wind's cooling late in the run.

Altitude. The body must have oxygen to keep running, and up in the mountains there is less of it. This becomes apparent at elevations above 2000 or 3000 feet, and grows more dramatic the higher you go. Breathing is more difficult than usual. The heart pounds harder. Hills and fast pace require more effort. You may dehydrate quicker.

On first exposure to high elevations, plan to cut back on distance, pace, or both for several days. Adaptation takes one to two weeks or more. Then comes the benefit. You'll notice that you run easier and faster than normal when you return to sea level after an extended stay at altitude. Your oxygen-supply system has super-compensated for the thin air by manufacturing extra red blood cells.

The Earth

A running-magazine survey has unmasked a running myth—one that says pounding along on hard surfaces is most likely to produce injuries, while soft surfaces such as grass and dirt are kindest to the feet and legs.

The *Runner's World* study of thousands of runners indicated that grass/dirt runners got hurt just as often as those who ran entirely on asphalt/concrete. The conclusion was that errors in the running routine are more likely to cause problems than the running surface.

Improvements in shoes have neutralized much of the pounding, and most runners now use the roads for several reasons. The streets generally are well-lighted for running at any hour; they are runnable in all weather conditions; they offer sure, smooth footing.

While practicalities dictate that much of your running will be on hard surfaces, don't deprive yourself completely of the softer ones. The statistics ignore one key fact. The minor aches (as opposed to true injuries) from constant pounding are clearly greater on hard road surfaces, and the soft ones are more pleasing aesthetically.

Hilly terrain makes for hard running whether the surface is soft or unyielding. David Costill, Ph.D., the sport's leading physiologist, says, "Hilly terrain will significantly impair a runner's performance." Even with an equal amount of climbing and descending, there is a large net drain on energy compared to flat runs.

This is no news to you if you have run up a hill. You don't need a physiologist (or a poet like Shakespeare, who wrote, "These high, wild hills and rough uneven ways draw out the miles and make them wearisome") to tell you what hills do to your legs and wind.

Hills are a stress that a beginner doesn't need. They add extra stresses which he or she isn't yet prepared to handle. Hills send pulse and breathing rates to their peaks, destroying any value in heart-rate monitoring and "talk-tests" as controls of effort. Hills, both up and down, also put extra strain on legs which still aren't fully conditioned.

As a general rule, runners should stay off the hills completely until they can run a half-hour comfortably on the flat. After graduating to hills, give them the respect they deserve. They shrink for no one, so you have to do the adapting.

Downhill. Absorb the added shock by keeping center of gravity low and landing with exaggerated flex of knees. Look down to promote a forward lean.

Uphill. Keep effort constant by slowing pace somewhat. Lean into the hill, concentrating on pumping harder with the arms and "lifting" with the knees and ankles.

Figure 8.4 Uphill and Downhill

How to adapt? By changing your running form. For uphill and downhill running, the form is much different than on the flat (see Chapter 14). Adjust for hills the way you would if you were riding a ten-speed bicycle on hilly terrain. You know you can't ride up in the same gear all the way. You have to shift, pump, coast, and brake in tune with the hills, all the while maintaining a constant pedaling rate.

Shift to lower "gears" while going uphill. Cut the stride length. Lean forward. Try to keep the *effort* rather constant, not the pace.

Freewheel while going downhill in higher "gear." Lean forward slightly to take advantage of gravity. But stay under some control. Don't be too proud to do some braking.

The Negatives

Distractions and Dangers

George Shechan, M.D., once remarked with tongue only partly in cheek that runners have three natural enemies: "dogs, drivers, and doctors." He explained that each group seems bent on taking running away from the runner. Dogs attack, drivers rule the roads, and some doctors say, "It hurts to run? Then don't run."

Fortunately, the medical profession has come to realize that what runners want most is to keep running. Led by men such as Dr. Sheehan, doctors now provide solid information on avoiding and treating injuries, rather than dispensing simplistic "stop-running" advice.

This one "enemy" is now converted to friend. But that still leaves us with two others plus an additional group that Sheehan didn't mention: the human adversary, who sometimes wears the disguise of an ally.

Dogs, drivers, and related distractions and dangers are discussed later in this chapter. First, however, the subject is how to live in peace other runners. Well-meaning though you and they might be, you might spoil each other's fun with careless actions and remarks.

How to make yourself unpopular with fellow runners:

- Claim the inside lane of the track as your own, never moving as faster people run extra distance in order to pass.
- Assume that you are superior to slower runners and that they must always get out of your way.
- Stay two steps ahead of a slower partner, and talk condescendingly over your shoulder or as you run backwards.
- Choose partners much faster than yourself, then make them wait for you while you stop and catch your breath.
- Agree to meet someone for an early-morning run at a distant location, then don't show up.
- Make every run a race, and sprint the last few yards of a run so you can brag, "I beat you."
- Ask about another runner's progress, then respond to the answer by saying, "Is that all you're doing?"
- Exaggerate your own distances and times.
- Offer unsolicited critiques of the other person's running style, clothing, and shoes.
- Talk as if you are the source of all running wisdom and your listener knows nothing, even though you're both studying the same publications at the same time.

Dogs and People

It would be wrong to plant the idea here that everyone on the street views you as a potential target for insults. Of every hundred people you pass, one might throw out an obnoxious taunt like "Hut, two, three, four!" or "Faster, faster!" One might wish you well with a, "Hang in there." The other ninety-eight simply don't notice you or don't care.

Still, for people first starting to run in public, it's normal to feel conspicuous and hypersensitive toward criticism. New runners think everyone is staring at them and pointing out their shortcomings. This feeling passes. But at first, even the isolated hostile or sarcastic remark can be enough to drive the new runner back undercover.

Unfortunately, the rare heckler is persistent. The best way to deal with these taunts is to bite your lip and ignore them. Responding in anger, with a sharp word or an obscene gesture, is exactly the kind of response the heckler wanted to provoke. Your next-best weapon is humor. A carefully chosen retort can defuse the hostilities on both sides and turn them into smiles.

The heckler is in a class with the dog. Some quirk in the nature of both turns them nasty at the sight of a runner. The difference is that a dog can't help itself. It acts on instinct.

A dog is cute and funny and lovable—as long as it is yours. When you unwittingly cross a dog's territorial lines, it may do a Jekyll-Hyde act and become a beast intent on removing portions of your well-trained legs. Dogs are bred to protect their property lines against all intruders.

Dogs also are natural cowards. They will attack when they sense fear, but they very rarely will engage in combat with a human who doesn't run away. A runner's best defense, then, is a strong offense.

- Don't try to run away. This only provokes the dog, and you can't outrun anything faster than a basset hound. If a dog makes menacing gestures at you, slow down, walk, or stop. Keep it in front of you; never let it get an unguarded shot at your backside if you value your flesh.
- Take the offensive. Look the dog straight in the eye, point at it, and answer in kind. Growl, "Get back there!" or more original epithets—anything to frighten the animal. Noise inspires fear, which stops most attacks. (Few experiences in running are more satisfying than seeing a dog turn and race away, yelping.)
- If noise doesn't work, try a weapon. Reach down for a stick or stone. Even an imaginary one often is enough. The simple act of reaching may cause a dog to give up the chase because instinct tells it that man is dangerous when armed.

Remember, too, that friendly dogs can also cause trouble. A hyperactive puppy can dance around and tangle itself in your legs. Don't take your eyes off any dog, even one that is wagging its tail.

Cars and Drivers

Streets and roads are convenient places to run, and you probably do much of your running there. They offer smooth, weather-proof surfaces. In town, the streets are lighted for early-morning and late-evening runs. Eventually, every runner hits the roads for this convenience, and in doing so courts their dangers.

Running in traffic is by far the greatest danger a runner faces. Look at the odds: You take perhaps 150 pounds of soft flesh to the road and travel less than eight miles an hour. The automobile weighs more than ten times that much, may travel ten times as fast, and is made of hard metal. When runner meets car, it's obvious which one wins.

Dozens of times a year, runners are killed or maimed in traffic. Yet other runners don't recognize the seriousness of the threat. They worry about distances and paces, while ignoring the deadly menace hurtling past every few seconds, two feet from their elbows.

The Insurance Institute for Highway Safety analyzed sixty runner/auto accidents occurring during a one-year period. Half of the runners died of their injuries. When police assessed the blame for the sixty collisions, nearly half were equally the fault of the driver and the runner. Nineteen cases were charged to runner error and sixteen to the driver.

Questions of blame are academic, and the idea that the pedestrian has the right of way is strictly a legal principle when hard metal meets soft skin. Many runners wind up dead right.

Table 9.1 *Rules of the Road*

Caution: The roads may be hazardous to your health. If you must run there, observe these common-sense precautions:

1. Always yield the right of way. The roads belong to the vehicles, and they are much bigger than you are. Don't challenge them for space because you'll lose any argument.

2. Run defensively and with a hint of paranoia. Assume that all drivers are out to get you, and don't give them that chance.

3. Stay awake. Runners have a tendency to daydream away the miles, but you can't afford this luxury on a busy street. Keep your head up and your eyes on the road.

4. Be seen, particularly when running in the dark. Wear brightly colored clothing in the daytime, reflective items at night.

5. See what's coming. Wear a visor or billed cap in darkness to shade your eyes from headlights which could blind you. (Drivers rarely dim their lights for oncoming runners.)

6. Be most careful at sunrise and sunset. Several factors make these the most dangerous hours: rush-hour traffic, sleepy or exhausted commuters, and the glare of the low sun in the driver's or the runner's eyes.

7. Run on the right, facing traffic—except when that side of the street offers little running room and the left appears safer. On lightly traveled, narrow roads, the best path may actually be down the middle. That way, you can quickly move to either side.

8. Don't forget bicycles and motorcycles. They travel almost as fast as cars, are less visible, and can inflict great damage—both to you and the rider.

9. Don't provoke drivers by invading their lane, darting out in front of them, or pounding their cars in cases of close calls. You never know when a driver might be drunk or emotionally unbalanced.

10. Report serious incidents. Take license numbers if a driver intentionally swerves to force you off the road or a passenger aims a missile at your head. Runners have charged "assault with a deadly weapon" and won.

Right. In normal circumstances, run on the left, facing oncoming traffic. Allow a "safety margin" of a sidewalk, shoulder or bike lane.

Wrong. Running with oncoming traffic to the rear, on a road without an adequate safety margin (sidewalk, shoulder or bike lane).

Figure 9.1 Traffic Safety

Personal Attacks

Men occasionally come under attack. Stories appear every so often in running magazines about a lone male being set upon by a young hoodlums with nothing better to do than beat up a defenseless runner. Yet a man on the run is probably safer than he would be if he walked slowly through the same neighborhood. A burst of speed usually leaves the troublemakers behind.

Most attackers choose women as targets for verbal and even physical abuse. These incidents are distressingly common, and their consequences can be quite serious.

RunHers, a women's running club in Washington, D.C., reported shocking data on threats and attacks directed at its members. Of ninety-nine women questioned, forty-one reported one or more incidents. Most of these were verbal harassment, but more than one-quarter of the cases involved being chased or grabbed.

Laura MacKenzie, who compiled the report, asserts, "No area is completely safe; vigilance is always prudent. However, some types of areas are considerably safer than others."

Neighborhoods are safest. RunHers members ran thirty-eight percent of their miles in residential areas, but only sixteen percent of the incidents occurred there.

The risk increases on bike paths. These were the scene of twenty-five percent of the problems, while these women ran there twenty-one percent of the time.

Parks are most dangerous. Only six percent of running was done in secluded parklands, but this accounted for twenty-seven percent of the threats and attacks.

This report points out the greatest inequity in running: Men can run almost anywhere, anytime, while the best running areas aren't always available to a woman alone.

Women fight back several ways. They run together for safety in numbers, they run with a man, or they carry weapons such as chemical sprays. All systems work, but none is entirely satisfactory. Perhaps the best solution is to run with a big dog. The dog gets exercise, and you feel safer.

"I haven't had a single comment from a guy since I began running with my doberman pinscher," says one woman who had been bothered frequently. "The main thing dogs have going for them as partners that people don't is the dog will run at your time and your convenience, your pace and your distance, without expecting you to carry on witty conversation."

THE RUNNING CONSUMER

*R*unning isn't what it used to be. In little more than a decade, it has evolved from small to large, simple to complex, cheap to potentially quite expensive.

Runners who remember the sport as it was before Frank Shorter won the 1972 Olympic Marathon may mourn the passing of an era when they could greet everyone at races by first name; when they could write all they needed to know about training on a three-by-five card; when they could equip themselves for running with a $20 bill.

I miss some of that smallness and simplicity, too, but I have no desire to return to the age of innocence, circa 1960. Return with me now for a non-nostalgic tour of the not-so-thrilling days of yesteryear.

- Almost no one younger than fourteen or older than twenty-two did any running. You rarely saw a woman on the road. The only reason to run was to train for racing. The only reason to race was to finish first and set records. The only excuse for continued running and racing was that you hoped to climb higher on the competitive ladder.
- The Boston Marathon drew only a few hundred runners, and there weren't half a dozen other races at this distance nationwide. The Bay to Breakers was still called the "Cross-City Race," and, with only a few dozen runners, it was in danger of extinction. The term "10-K" hadn't yet been coined; neither had "fun-run."

- You usually trained on the track—always hard, always under the watch, and usually under a coach from the "pain equals gain" school. A "long" run was anything longer than your short racing distance. A "slow" run was anything slower than your fast racing pace. You seldom ran—or were able to run—more than twenty-five miles weekly.
- When you got hurt, the only advice your heard was either "rest it" or "run it off." Your shoes were made of leather or canvas, and weren't designed for distance running. You wore the spiked shoes of a sprinter, without heels, and felt like you were always running uphill. Your flats didn't have any heel lift, either, and they were castoffs from tennis or basketball. You ordered shoes by mail, never sure you'd get the size or style you wanted.
- Your choice of magazine was either *Track and Field News* (which, then as now, did a superb job of reporting track; but, unlike now, ignored off-track running) or *Long Distance Log,* which was the sport's best-kept secret. If you wanted a book, you ordered it from one source—*T&FN*—and the selections and their practical value were limited.
- Hardly a run went by without someone shouting, "Hup-two-three!" as you passed. You heard, "Why are you out in your underwear?" in summer, and, "Why are you out in your pajamas?" in winter. You ran in the dark to avoid hecklers. You tried to hide the fact that you were a runner.

Tell me about the "good old days," and I'll give you dozens of reasons why the best time to be a runner is the present. Running isn't what it used to be, and for that we can all rejoice.

We have left an era of limits, when the runner had to make do with what little was available in equipment, information, and opportunity. We now live in an era of choices, when the runner is required to select wisely among a wide variety of options.

Most of the new expenses and complications are optional. A runner can buy or do almost anything, but still *needs* very little.

The Equipment

Shoes and Clothes

Running is not a style show. At least it doesn't need to be, although it sometimes appears that way in the era of $100 running shoes and even more status-conscious designer "jogging suits."

What are the essentials? Good shoes and whatever else feels comfortable. Dress for function, not fashion; for comfort and according to the conditions, not to draw attention; for protection and concealment, not for show.

One of the beauties of running as a sport or exercise is its low cost. It can be a very inexpensive activity. Don't neutralize that advantage by outfitting yourself as if you were on your way to the ski slopes.

A few rules for dressing up to run:

- Splurge on good shoes—*running* shoes, not those designed for other sports. These are rather expensive and are growing more so. But they are a most important investment, not a luxury. Your health and performance rest on your feet, so protect them well. Plan on spending about $50 for a good pair of shoes, and to replace them at least once a year. Your feet and legs will thank you. This annual $100 or so should be your only major, recurring equipment expenditure.

- Keep the rest of your wardrobe simple and inexpensive. Use what you now have in your drawers and closets. Improvise instead of running up a clothing bill. Sure, the fancy "jogging suits" look nice; by all means wear one if you already own it. But this is a luxury costing as much as two pairs of shoes. Any loose-fitting, non-chafing shirts, and long pants or shorts will work almost as well.
- Dress inconspicuously. This advice applies mainly to beginners, who already feel all eyes are on them. They'll feel better about running in public if their clothing doesn't draw special attention or show off bulges that they want to hide.
- Don't overdress. The tendency among people inexperienced with running at the extremes of climate is to dress as if they're going to sit outside and watch a football game. They feel toasty warm at the start. But they heat up inside as they run and soon wish they'd left half the clothing at home. Leave half of it there before you go out, or dress in layers (for instance, a jacket over a sweater over a T-shirt on a cold day) which can easily be stripped off en route.
- Avoid short-cut weight reduction gimmicks. Don't wear a rubberized suit or uncomfortably heavy clothing, imagining you'll lose weight that way. You'll lose *sweat,* and your body temperature will soar. But nothing will happen to your true weight that wouldn't have happened without this wrapping. Lose weight the natural, safe way—with sensible exercise and diet—not by sweating yourself dry.

Choosing Shoes

What do you look for in shoes? First, consider your needs. You probably are running modest distances at modest paces, not trying to break four minutes in the mile or run ultramarathons. If you're just starting to run, you may be somewhat heavier than you'd prefer. Your feet and legs may not yet be conditioned to tolerate the pounding inflicted by hard surfaces.

Therefore, look for well-cushioned, well-supported (but not excessively so) shoes with the following features: a soft, non-irritating upper material (nylon or suede is softer than standard leather); adequate toe room (a function of size and the cut of the shoe); firm sole material on the outside for durability and a softer midsole for comfort; heel lift (a "wedge" which raises the heel about a half-inch higher than the sole) and heel protection (in the form of a rigid "counter" around the back for stability); and forefoot flexibility (so the foot can bend easily).

Many well-established manufacturers stand ready to fill these needs. In alphabetical order, the ten best-selling brands are Adidas, Brooks, Converse, Etonic, New Balance, Nike, Puma, Reebok, Saucony, and Tiger. Choose shoes from these companies, and you can't go far wrong. Examine the properties of other brands more closely.

Prices vary enormously. You can pick up minor brands in discount stores for less than $20, and you can splurge on high-tech models that cost $100 or more. Avoid both extremes. You can protect yourself quite well on name-brand shoes costing $30 to $50. Ask the advice of an experienced runner or a sympathetic shoe salesperson on matters of selection and fit.

Another consideration: your foot type. Doctors specializing in foot health categorize feet in two general ways: "floppy" and "rigid." The first tends to be flat, while the second shows extremely high arches. The floppy foot needs greater stability (the tradeoffs are reduced cushioning and flexibility) from shoes and usually responds best to a model with a straight last. The rigid foot requires more cushioning, more flexibility, and often a curved last (see Figure 10.1).

The first step in avoiding injury is making the right shoe choice. The second step is not letting these shoes wear out too much. All shoes break down from hard use, losing cushioning and support as well as sole material. The critical factor is excessive wear at the heels. Most runners grind down their heels slightly to the outside of center. This gradually tips the footplant out of balance. When a quarter- to a half-inch of rubber is gone, the unusual forces can become troublesome. Consider repairing or replacing the shoes when they reach this condition.

What Else to Wear

How do you know how much clothing is enough? Check the weather reports, and add or subtract items depending on how hot or cold the day is.

This advice might be too obvious to mention, except that the temperatures on the thermometer are not what they seem when you run. What felt like comfortable weather at the start soon becomes warm, and later hot.

The "Twenty-Degree Rule" applies to running. This rule states that the perceived temperature automatically rises by that much in the course of a run. So a nice, sunny, seventy-degree afternoon soon feels like a steamy ninety; a chilling, thirty-degree evening becomes a pleasant fifty; a bitterly cold, ten-degree morning becomes a tolerable thirty.

Dress with the "Twenty-Degree Rule" in mind. Generally speaking, a hot day for running is one when the temperature exceeds seventy, warm is in the fifty to sixty range, cool is just above freezing through the high forties, and cold is below freezing. (These figures are, of course, skewed by the effects of high humidity in hot weather and the wind-chill factor on cold days, which are discussed in Chapter 8.)

Start dressing each day from a foundation of underwear, socks, shoes, and shorts. Add layers from a basic wardrobe, including a sleeveless tank top (for hot days), long pants and long-sleeved shirt (for cool weather), jacket, gloves, and stocking cap (for cold conditions).

Rain needn't stop a run. Just add a baseball-style cap to keep the water off your face, wear rain-repelling clothing if the day is cool, and splash away. Think of it this way: You're already wet from sweat, so the rain can't make you much wetter.

Abundant Accessories

What more might you need? Not much, although lots of manufacturers would like to have you sample their products.

A typical issue of a running magazine carries advertising for watches which measure your pulse rate and establish a tempo for your runs, weighted gloves to increase your arm

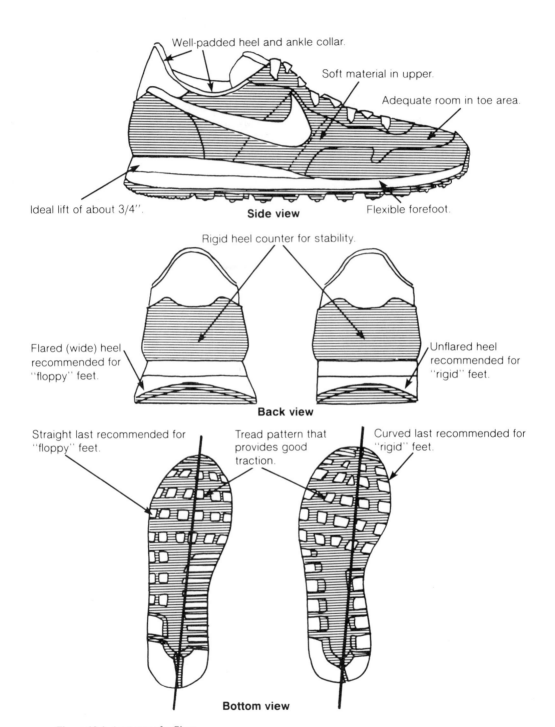

Well-padded heel and ankle collar.

Soft material in upper.

Adequate room in toe area.

Ideal lift of about 3/4''.

Side view

Flexible forefoot.

Rigid heel counter for stability.

Flared (wide) heel recommended for ''floppy'' feet.

Unflared heel recommended for ''rigid'' feet.

Back view

Straight last recommended for ''floppy'' feet.

Tread pattern that provides good traction.

Curved last recommended for ''rigid'' feet.

Bottom view

Figure 10.1 Anatomy of a Shoe

Table 10.1 *Dressing for the Day*

Remember your "Twenty-Degree Rule." The air temperature seems to rise by about that amount when you run. Dress with that warming trend in mind. Start from the basis of shoes, running shorts, and underwear; then add layers according to the conditions.

Perceived Condition	Actual Temperature	Clothing to Wear
Hot	70s and up	Add only the skimpiest singlet (tank top) that modesty will allow; men may choose to go shirtless.
Warm	50s and 60s	Add a short-sleeved T-shirt to the basic uniform.
Cool	30s and 40s	Add long pants and a long-sleeved shirt or light jacket.
Cold	20s and down	Add a layer of protection for hands and ears, and perhaps another layer for legs and face in extreme cold.
Rain	Warm	Add a cap with a bill to keep vision clear; otherwise dress as on any warm day.
Rain	Cool	Add a cap plus a water-repelling jacket and pants; don't wear cotton "sweats" which soak up water.
Snow	Cold	Add extra socks to keep feet warm and dry; be sure the shoes provide adequate traction on slippery roads.

strength while you run, belts with pouches for liquids in case you get thirsty on the road, stereo headsets complete with tapes specifically designed for the runner, key carriers, identification tags, and personalized headbands. The list goes on and on.

While applauding the ingenuity of American businesspeople, I urge you to treat most of these items only as curiosities. They add little to your running, and in some cases might detract from it. However, four groups of accessories do contribute significantly to your running health and enjoyment.

1. A digital watch with a stopwatch feature measure your running times accurately. These watches, commonly made of black plastic, come under several brand names, and their prices have dropped markedly in recent years. Twenty dollars should get you all the watch you need.

2. Several commercial products allow you to extend the life of your running shoes. Simply spread the glue-like material on worn-out heels, mold it into the original shape of the heel, and allow it to harden. This product may be both a money-saver and a leg-saver.
3. If you're having trouble with your feet and legs, you may want to experiment with inside-the-shoe products. These range from shock-absorbing heel pads to slip-in arch supports that provide more protection than those built into the shoes. Custom-made shoe inserts, designed by a specialist, should only be considered if you're suffering chronic foot or leg pain.
4. Nighttime runners, take heed: You're almost invisible on the dark streets unless you wear some type of reflective material. This may be as simple as strips of luminous tape on your shoes and clothing, or as fancy as a reflective vest or jacket made specifically for running. It can't be repeated too often that drivers are the biggest danger a runner ever faces.

The
Resources

Alone and Together

"The loneliness of long-distance runner." This phrase has endured as a cliché ever since Allan Sillitoe wrote a short novel and later a screenplay by that title in the 1960s. The story was fiction, and so is the usual usage of the word "lonely" as it applies to long-distance runners.

Don't feel sorry for the lone runner. This apparent loneliness is neither a negative factor nor a necessary evil of the activity. Many runners *prefer* to run by themselves; this may be the only chance they have all day to escape the crowds that press in upon them, and the voices that assault their ears at home, at work, or at school. The solitude is self-sought.

On the other hand, a runner who who wants this to be a more sociable activity can plug into a very active support system. This is among the friendliest of sports—perhaps because there is little person-versus-person competition, perhaps because the act of running itself breaks down certain barriers to communiction.

Thaddeus Kostrubala, M.D., was among the first psychiatrists to use running as a therapeutic tool. He says patients bare their souls more completely after at least a half-hour's run than at any other time. Long-time runners will tell you only half-jokingly that running develops one set of muscles more thoroughly than any other: those that operate the mouth. Those same muscles are also the last to tire.

What every runner most enjoys doing is talking about himself or herself, so you can instantly strike up conversations with strangers who run by asking, "How is your running going?" The flattering question you can ask a runner is, "Can you give me some advice?" Don't be afraid to ask; just be prepared for long answers.

The compulsion to talk about running is nearly matched by the urge to write about it. Most runners keep diaries that preserve their statistics and experiences in loving detail (see Chapter 21). Many writers make their observations public in magazines and books.

More than a dozen national magazines, and ten times that many local and regional publications, regularly cover running in the United States from every imaginable perspective. Hundreds of books have been published in this field, with new ones appearing on the shelves each year.

If nothing else, the readership of these publications shows that you have lots of friends who share your running joys and problems.

Organizations

Running in an organized way doesn't imply joining super-serious racers. Organizations have something to offer runners at every level, if only to give a "we're-in-this-together" feeling to people who otherwise might think they're running in isolation.

Organizations, local to national, welcome runners of all abilities and ambitions. Colleges, adult-education programs, recreation departments, YMCAs and the like offer excellent beginning-running instruction in most communities. If you're starting, ask about existing groups in your city.

More advanced runners may wish to join a local running club. These usually are informal gatherings, open to runners of all abilities and ambitions. You probably won't find the clubs listed in a phone book, so ask other runners about them.

Races exist within easy driving distance of nearly everyone, and most of these events require no racing experience or talent of their entrants. Watch your area's newspaper for an announcement of a race you might run. Once you get there, you'll hear about several more to come.

Nationally, three organizations cater to grassroots runners. All offer publications and awards programs.

- American Running and Fitness Association
  2420 K Street, NW
  Washington, DC 20037
- President's Council on Physical Fitness and Sports
  Washington, DC 20025
- Road Runners Club of America
  c/o Harold Tinsley
  8811 Edgehill Drive
  Huntsville, AL 35802

At the peak of the organizational pyramid rests The Athletic Congress, the national governing body for track, cross-country, and road racing. TAC and its regional affiliates sanction most of the country's major running events, make the rules, certify the courses, and keep the records of the sport. For information on membership, write to the national office, Box 120, Indianapolis, IN 46206.

Periodicals

This is by no means a complete list of running magazines and newsletters, but these are the most established of the national publications.

- General interest: *Runner* (1 Park Avenue, New York, NY 10016) and *Runner's World* (33 East Minor Street, Emmaus, PA 18049). These glossy, colorful, mass-circulation magazines are found on most newsstands.
- Racing-oriented: *Running Times* (14416 Jefferson Davis Highway, Number 20, Woodbridge, VA 22191) and *RRCA Footnotes* (11155 Saffold Way, Reston, VA 22090). These publications are intended for the reader whose running has achieved a certain degree of seriousness.
- High-level competition: *Track and Field News* (Box 296, Los Altos, CA 94022) and *Women's Track and Field World* (Box 850, Cedar Glen, CA 92321). These magazines are directed more toward the fan than the participant.
- Women's running: *Women's Sports and Fitness* (310 Town and Country Village, Palo Alto, CA 94301). This is an all-sports magazine with heavy emphasis on running.
- Masters running: *Master Runner* (1210 Seventh Street, Southeast, Number C-23, Washington, DC 20003) and *National Masters News* (Box 2372, Van Nuys, CA 91404). These publications are runners who have passed their thirtieth birthday.
- Newsletters: *Jeff Galloway's Running Advice* (576 Armour Circle, Atlanta, GA 30324); *Running Stats,* (1310 College Avenue, Number 1081, Boulder, CO 80302); *Run and FitNews* (2420 K Street, Northwest, Washington, DC 20037). *Running Commentary* (4620 Manzanita Street, Eugene, OR 97405). These cover the latest news and technical develpments.

Recommended Books

Of the dozens of books spawned by the running boom, these are my favorites (among those published through 1984), along with capsule reviews.

- All-purpose: *The Complete Book of Running* by James F. Fixx (Random House, 1977). This is running's all-time best-seller and deservedly so.
- Basic: *Beginner's Running Guide* by Hal Higdon (Anderson/World, 1978). This is a collection of wisdom from Higdon's thirty-year career as a running writer.

- Advanced: Tie between *Galloway's Book of Running* by Jeff Galloway (Shelter Publications, 1984) and *Serious Runner's Handbook* by Tom Osler (Anderson/World, 1978). These men are two of the sport's geniuses.
- Women: *Women's Running* by Joan L. Ullyot, M.D. (Anderson/World, 1976). This was the first of the women's books and is still the best.
- Marathoning: *The Marathon* by Marc Bloom (Holt, Reinhart and Winston, 1981). This volume is a Fixx-like effort, covering the "Everest" of races.
- Ultramarathoning: *The Ultimate Challenge* by Tom Osler and Ed Dodd (Anderson/World, 1979). This is another of Osler's important contributions to running thought and technique.
- Triathloning: *Triathlon* by Sally Edwards (Contemporary Books, 1983). Edwards's work is one of the first books on the subject by an early triathlete.
- General fitness: The *Aerobics* series by Kenneth H. Cooper, M.D. (M. Evans and Co., 1968 to 1982). Cooper gave aerobic fitness a scientific foundation.
- Physiology: *A Scientific Approach to Distance Running* by David L. Costill, Ph.D. (Tafnews Press, 1978). He put science into high-performance running.
- Medicine: *Medical Advice for Runners* by George A. Sheehan, M.D. (Anderson/World, 1978). This book is like having the doctor himself make housecalls.
- History: *Fast Tracks—the History of Distance Running* by Raymond Krise and William Squires (Stephen Greene Press, 1982). The full story of the oldest sport is presented here.
- Psychology: *The Joy of Running* by Thaddeus Kostrubala, M.D. (Pocket Books, 1977). This book examines the theories and practices of the pioneering runner/psychiatrist.
- Philosophy: *Dr. Sheehan on Running* by George A. Sheehan, M.D. (Bantam Books, 1978). This book offers answers to the *whys* of running.
- Biography: *Running Back* by Steve Heidenreich with David Dorr (Hawthorn, 1979). This book recounts a world-class miler's inspiring return from a near-fatal accident.
- Fiction: *Once a Runner* by John L. Parker, Jr. (Cedarwinds Press, 1978). This fictitious account captures running as it truly is.
- Humor: *On the Run from Dogs and People* by Hal Higdon (Chicago Review Press, 1979). Higdon offers a rare chance for us to laugh at ourselves and our sport.

This list doesn't include many of the classics—those groundbreaking books written before 1970. Few people ever got to read them, and most of these books are long out of print. But their authors still deserve to be recognized for inspiring later generations of writers.

- *How They Train* by Fred Wilt (Tafnews Press, 1958). This collection of training data was published at a time when no one knew enough about the subject.
- *Run to the Top* by Arthur Lydiard with Garth Gilmour (Minerva, 1962). This book set off a revolution in training.
- *The Conditioning of Distance Runners* by Tom Osler (*Long Distance Log,* 1966). Never has anyone said so much in just thirty-two pages.

- *Jogging* by Bill Bowerman and W. E. Harris (Grosset and Dunlap, 1967). This pre-Cooper text appeals to its readers to run for exercise.
- *What Research Tells the Coach About Distance Running* by David Costill, Ph.D. (AAPHER, 1968). This early publication attempted to make scientific sense of the sport.

For listings and reviews of more than 200 titles, consult the book *Running: A Guide to the Literature* by Bob Wischnia and Marty Post (Garland Publishing, 1983).

The Events

Races for Everyone

We've known since running first boomed that this is too good a sport to belong exclusively to those who run best. The major races lavish fame and fortune on their winners, while allowing huge numbers of runners with less talent but serious commitment to run along with them.

We're now learning that seriousness isn't even an entry requirement. An editorial in *Rocky Mountain Running News* notes: "A change has crept into the sport of road racing—not a revolution, more like an evolution. But for those who can recall those halcyon days before the 'craze' hit, it is clear that races are not what they used to be. Most racers today are loose and happy. Races have to be fun, fun, fun. Music, balloons and colorful pennants abound. Many races encourage costumes or award prizes for the oldest, youngest, tallest, slowest, most patriotic and best tandem. Race advertising tends to emphasize the frivolity rather than the competition of the event."

These events may not even be races in the traditional sense of the word. Some look more like mobile parties—the place to go on a Sunday in lieu of a trip to an amusement park. Nowhere is this more true than at the Bay to Breakers Run.

A survey taken at the 1984 San Francisco event produced numbers that might shock the sport's purists: thirty-eight percent of the runners trained less than ten miles a week, and twelve percent ran without training at all; one runner in eleven wore a Halloween-style costume.

The percentages translate to about 10,000 people who weren't trained runners, who treated Bay to Breakers as a masquerade ball, or both. Most of the other 70,000 or 80,000 men and women on the streets of San Francisco that day wouldn't have *raced* the twelve kilometers even without the human traffic jam. They were content to run the distance at everyday training pace.

Nothing is wrong with any of that. Bay to Breakers, Bloomsday in Spokane and Peachtree in Atlanta—the country's three largest running events—offer something for everyone. They feature invited celebrities, anonymous but serious racers behind them, people out for a good training run, and growing numbers of celebrants who wouldn't otherwise consider themselves "runners."

I agree with the *Rocky Mountain Running News* conclusion: "If adding splashes of color, a few painted clowns and a little Van Halen music will convince large crowds of people that running miles is fine, bring in the clowns."

I see these mass celebrations of running as a healthy antidote to the "wining is the only thing" thinking that once dominated this sport and still prevails in most other sports. However, I would not want to see this attitude evolve to "winning is *nothing*."

The running revolution is rooted in the idea that everyone can feel like a winner. Races wouldn't attract thousands of "losers." But even while we're trying to win in personal terms, we must recognize that some people are bigger winners than others.

Competition in the traditional sense, a man and a woman beating all other men and women, was never better. The stakes, now expressed openly in dollar terms, were never higher. You may say you don't know or care who finishes first, but that misses the point. The people who race for the top prizes care very much and work very hard to get where they are.

You may ask, "Do the races really need these pros?" Maybe not, but that, too, misses the point. The pros (who may approach their running professionally even if they're never paid) need the races to hone and display their talents. They need large crowds of lesser runners to make themselves look good.

I'll be bothered by the new direction road racing has taken only if the best of us and the rest of us can't continue to run together; only if the frivolous side of racing overwhelms the serious side; only if the new trend turns this proud old sport into a joke.

Changing Times

"Terrified," "horrified," and "concerned" were the words a columnist in Eugene, Oregon, attributed to runners in my hometown as they reviewed the events of late 1984. This writer thought he detected terror over what happened to Jim Fixx on a road in Vermont, horror over what happened to Gabriele Andersen on her way to the Olympic Marathon finish line, and concern over what didn't happen at a local marathon, where the field had shrunk by two-thirds in two years.

The Eugene columnist concluded, "Maybe it's time to ask the question: Has the running boom fizzled?"

Writers started asking this question shortly after Kenneth Cooper, M.D., fired the first shots of the running revolution. The answer was "no" in 1968, and it is still "no." Running is only changing, not fizzling.

Anyone who thinks otherwise doesn't know how adaptable to change we runners are. We are approaching the sport somewhat differently now than we did a few years ago. These changes are signs of running's health. If it were sick, it would be stagnant.

Some changes are dramatic, others are trivial. Some are of lasting significance, others are trendy and will soon yield to the next fad. I make no attempt to assign importance to what is happening. I just report on what appears to be coming in and going out in the mid-1980s.

People. There are fewer beginners than at any time since the mid-1970s but more "lifers" (runners who will never stop) than ever before. The period of spectacular growth in numbers has ended, but the sport continues to grow in sophistication as more people keep running longer. The percentage of runners from the school-age group shrinks, while women make up an ever-larger part of the running population. Fewer people are running zealots, and more runners have modified their obsession with the sport.

Training. More runners are running less often, while fewer of them are bragging about never missing a day. Recovery days are taken more frequently and with less guilt, while the hard days occur less often but are more intense because full recovery has taken place. The emphasis is more on quality and less on quantity; more on intervals and less on continuous running; more on running by daily time period and less on weekly mile-counting. Runners are doing more strength work and less stretching; more supplementing (primarily with bicycling and swimming) and less specializing in running; more training for a variety of races (including triathlons) and less peaking for a specific event.

Racing. Many races attract fewer doers and more viewers, as runners pass up chances to compete so they can watch their heroes. The emphasis on running marathons has declined, while the urge to improve times at shorter distances has increased. A smaller portion of the short races are 10-Ks, while the number of five-, eight-, and 12-Ks has grown. Fewer events call themselves "races," while more of them go by the name of "Run" or "Fun-Run" so as not to scare away the less-serious entrant. Serious runners demand more accuracy in course measurement and timing, and often receive less. The number of races is up, and the size of most fields is down.

Equipment. Everything runners wear is more stylish and less economical. Even at today's prices, shoes are a good investment, with companies offering more models that meet individual needs. Runners are wearing more long-sleeved and sleeveless shirts, and fewer T-shirts. You see more high-topped basketball shoes and low-cut football shoes for casual wear, and fewer running shoes. People on the roads wear more stereo headsets, and indulge in less conversation and contemplation.

Diet. Food faddism is less common, and more attention is paid to diets based on sound scientific evidence. Runners do less carbohydrate loading and eat more complex-carbos all the time. They do less feasting and more fasting (eating less than usual, at any rate) the night before races. They take fewer special drinks during and after races, and drink more water (during) and beer (after). Fewer of them are starving themselves for the sake of performance, and more are allowing their weight to climb to more comfortable levels.

Attitudes. Runners are more realistic in their thinking about what running can do for them. They take fewer risks in their approach to training and racing. They plan less for short-term success and more for long-term health and happiness.

Watching versus Doing

I was neither glad nor sad to see the 1984 Olympics end, because I didn't get involved enough to work up strong feelings either way. Sure, I watched the televised events from Los Angeles with more than a little interest, but from a safe physical and emotional distance. A trip to Munich twelve years earlier had put my priorities in order.

My Olympic hero from 1972 wasn't Frank Shorter or Lasse Viren. It was Tom Johnson. We hadn't known each other before arriving in Germany with a tour group, and we haven't met again since. I've never told Tom how much his quiet example meant to me.

Before the flight overseas, Johnson had never been inside an airplane. He'd never traveled more than 100 miles from his home in Washington, D.C., where he worked nights as an editorial artist for the *Post*. He described himself as "something of a hermit."

As Tom waited to board his plane, he wore only his running shorts, training shoes, and a T-shirt. He carried a small backpack.

"Where's your luggage?" the tour leader asked.

"This is it," Johnson replied as he tapped the pack. He brought only the necessities: a shaving kit, a change of running wear, sweat pants, nylon windbreaker, and a single dress shirt for "formal occasions."

If the clothing gave him an eccentric image, his actions on the plane added to it. Claustrophobia gripped him, and he paced the aisles of the 747 throughout the overnight flight.

No one saw much of Tom after we arrived in the village of Eisenartz, 100 kilometers by road but half a world away in style from the Olympic city of Munich. He spent his days on extended walk/run tours of the trails through the alpine foothills and along the Traun River.

"You know," he told me, "this is the first time I've ever been able to relax while I'm running. Here, I don't have to worry about getting mugged."

Mercedes buses carried the tour group to Munich and back each day. Johnson went along only three times, and not at all after the final races had started. The bus rides and the crowds at Olympic Stadium made him uneasy. Whatever he wanted to see, TV could show him. But his days on the trails didn't leave much time for televiewing.

"How can you be this close to the Games and then not watch them?" Tom was asked repeatedly. He just smiled and shrugged, making no attempt to plead his case.

The Olympic Games are the world's biggest second-hand thrill show. Spectators outnumber participants millions to one. Too many eyes focus on too few runners. Too many people care too much about events over which they have no control.

I did my share of reaching and grabbing for vicarious thrills at Munich and before. But that ended in September 1972, when I left behind forever the spectator's role of pseudo-involvement. I quit expecting other runners to provide thrills for me, quit imagining that their joys and pains belonged to anyone but themselves.

With three days remaining in those Olympics—the best three days for a distance fan—I sold my tickets at cost and quit taking the daily bus rides to and from Eisenartz. I arrived late at a place where Tom Johnson had been all along.

On a foggy morning, I ran along a river so clear I could see trout swimming at its bottom. Farmers were out early, raking hay by hand. Whole families walked the trail, and as we met they stepped aside, nodded, and mouthed, *"Guten Morgen."*

I spent most of the run smiling. I felt relaxed and in control of my emotions for the first time since the opening ceremonies.

The words of Juha Vaatainen, a great Finnish runner of that era, sprang to mind: "I enjoy the applause but realize it is temporary. I long to discover new faces, but I also like solitude. Stadiums were invented for spectators, not for runners. We have nature, and that's much better. Perhaps I like running so much because I am sort of a loner."

Olympic stadiums and Olympic marathon courses are the freeways of the sport. I've sat in enough of those stadiums and stood beside enough of those courses to know I'm much happier on the backroads—uncrowded, unhurried, unnoticed.

On the last day in Eisenartz, Tom Johnson refilled his backpack and boarded the Mercedes bus on the first lap of his trip home. Many of the tour members were tired and frustrated by the whole Olympic experience, sick of traveling and fighting crowds and living with the memories of the non-athletic tragedy of Munich. Tom looked contented. I asked him how he'd liked his trip.

"It was the greatest experience of my life," he said. "In fact, I'm planning to come back here next year for a vacation."

There wouldn't be any Olympics in 1973, but Johnson didn't need them to make his experiences great.

THE RUNNING EXERCISE

*T*he occasion was a mandatory health-education class for college freshmen. The topic was fitness. I recited without conviction the statistical indictment of these students' age-group, and they listened without being moved.

Two recent studies had concluded that the fitness of American youth was disgraceful. Two-thirds of teenagers couldn't meet minimum standards of speed and endurance, strength and flexibility. As a group, they were three percent fatter and much slower in a mile run than a similar group had been a few years earlier.

I didn't point a holier-than-thou finger at these young people. I first admitted that, in the ways the researchers had measured fitness, I wasn't very fit at their age and had grown less so.

I entered the Army in good enough running shape to threaten the Fort Jackson record for the one-mile test. But I failed three of the other four fitness tests and barely passed the fourth. I was only trained to run.

Today I'm at least three percent fatter than I was then, can do even fewer pushups and situps, and now run a minute per mile slower at all distances. That doesn't concern me. I'm still fit enough to do what I want physically, which is to run daily for a half-hour or more.

"Want" is the operative word here. I *want* to run regularly and race occasionally. The running still feels good, the racing remains exciting—even at slower paces than before. I'd want to continue even if these activities did nothing for my fitness.

I told the students I could understand why fitness might not appeal to them. The problem lies in the way it has been marketed in recent years. Fitness has been sold like prescription drugs: bitter pills that must be swallowed because they are good for us. This medicine is taken for negative reasons: to correct something bad that has already happened or to keep something worse from happening later.

Many runners run for more positive reasons: the good feelings, the excitement. Aerobic fitness then becomes an automatic by-product of the activity and not an end in itself; a basis for athletic success but not what keeps runners running. Other forms of fitness may actually decline as more time is spent on the main activity.

In one specific way, runners are remarkably fit. A study by Dr. David Wrisley of Sinai Hospital in Detroit ranks three subdivisions of runners among the top ten endurance athletes. "Elite" competitors lead the pack. "Good" distance runners place fourth (behind cross-country skiers and competitive rowers). Ultramarathoners rank tenth.

However, if these specialists had been tested for other aspects of fitness such as strength and flexibility, their scores probably would have been laughably low. Most of them would have admitted that excessive running caused one or more disabling injuries.

The one-dimensional development of runners and the safety of running have been noted by some critics of the activity. The concern grows out of confusion over what this really is— an exercise or a sport. It can be either, but probably not both at once.

Exercisers seek a safe prescription for fitness, while athletes seek improvement in performance. Anyone running to stay healthy can do it by observing aerobics pioneer Dr. Kenneth Cooper's limit of a comfortably paced three miles, five days a week. Anyone trying to improve distances and speeds must run farther, faster, and more often—and accept the risks that go with greater effort.

Runners who race don't live as dangerously as football and hockey players, skiers and skydivers. But we do take chances with our health whenever we exceed safe limits—which we do willingly, even eagerly. The point of this sport, as with most other sports, is to see how far we can we can bend before we break. It is unrealistic, then, to judge the athlete by the health standards of the exerciser.

These are the tradeoffs. Running-as-sport might never be perfectly safe, and running-for-fitness can never be thoroughly satisfying. Exercise is seen as something we think we *need* to take, sport as something we *want* to do.

CHAPTER THIRTEEN

The
Start

Starting Lines

(Chapters 13 through 18 are written specifically for people who have just begun to run or are starting to race—and for experienced runners to pass along to beginners. A suggested basic running program is presented in Chapter 16.)

The longest step in becoming a runner is deciding to start—or more accurately, *return.* We all ran as children, and it isn't a skill we've lost completely with age. Still, despite the well-publicized benefits and popularity of this activity, relatively few adults take that first step back into running.

Those who have reached a certain age may admit that they should start exercising more. They may even promise they'll begin—tomorrow. This is the same tomorrow-that-never-comes when they'll start their diet, cut down on their smoking and drinking, reduce the number of hours spent facing the television, or drive slower and buckle their seatbelts.

Changing one's old ways means replacing a set of familiar and comfortable habits (in this case, a too-easy life) with a new and more active—but also unfamiliar and uncomfortable—set of actions. This is never easy.

The hardest part of starting to run is replacing one kind of inertia with another. You remember the laws of inertia: A body at rest tends to stay at rest, and a body in motion stays in motion. Those facts of physics apply to the physical act of running as well.

First the mind resists the motion and needs to be convinced of the new activity's value. You already have leapt that mental barrier. You already have listed your reasons for trying running: losing weight and looking better, gaining enough endurance and speed to enter races, conditioning for other sports, pursuing the elusive "runner's high."

Now you can concentrate on the physical barriers. A body accustomed to rest doesn't instantly spring into motion. No matter how willing the mind is, the body resists the early movements in the new direction. Demanding too much of yourself too soon invites an early and disheartening end to your running experiment.

The first few weeks and months as a runner are exciting and risky. This is when improvement can come most rapidly—or when you can be injured and discouraged most easily. Each step must be taken most carefully now.

The next few chapters lead you through an exciting and challenging break-in period. You'll learn how to solve common running problems, how to refine your running techniques and how to plan your own running one safe step at a time.

The Winner Inside

You may think that you aren't yet an athlete. You may protest that you don't look, think, or act like one. You don't ever want to compete to win as a runner, and you may even doubt right now that you have what it takes to be any kind of runner. So what, you may ask, does this activity have to offer you besides the long and rather dreary-sounding progression of steps toward physical fitness?

One hidden reward is an opportunity for any non-athlete to start winning right away and to keep winning indefinitely. It is said that every fat person carries inside a thin one struggling to get out. Inside every new runner waits a winner about to surface.

Time and distance let you win. No runner, not even an Olympic champion, can beat everyone all the time. None can set the ultimate record that never will be broken. But every runner has the chance to go longer or faster today than he or she did yesterday.

You don't have to beat anyone to win. You don't have to reach any arbitrary standards of perfection, like finishing a marathon or breaking the five-minute mile. You win simply by improving your own standards, however humble those might seem at first. And never are your opportunities for improvement greater than right now. Never will you gain so much, so quickly, from so little work.

The typical improvement curve in running climbs most steeply in the early months, then levels out gradually before plateauing years down the road. As runners come closer and closer to their own peak, they train harder and harder for smaller and smaller gains. You have an advantage over these longtime athletes because you can take giant steps forward on as little as one mile, three days a week.

Before you begin chasing such progress, assess your present abilities carefully and realistically, then set your distances and paces accordingly. Whatever those levels are now, you can count on running at least twice as far and a minute per mile faster—without working any harder—before this introductory course is through. That is winning in the truest sense of the word: the personal sense.

Self-Analysis

Choose the number under each of ten important fitness factors that best describes you. Then add up the total score in Table 13.1. The results give you a rough idea of where your starting line should be.

- *Cardiovascular health:* 3 = no history of heart or circulatory problems, including high blood pressure; 2 = past ailments have been pronounced "cured"; 1 = such problems exist but medical care is not required; 0 = under medical care for cardiovascular trouble. (Warning: If you have such a disease history or are older than thirty-five, enter this program only after receiving clearance from your doctor—and then only with close supervision by a fitness instructor.)
- *Injuries:* 3 = no current injury problems; 2 = some pain during activity but performance isn't affected significantly; 1 = level of activity is limited by the injury; 0 = unable to do any strenuous work. (Warning: If your injury is temporary, wait until it is cured before starting the program; if it is chronic, adjust the program to fit your limitations.)
- *Illnesses:* 3 = no current illnesses; 2 = some problems during activity but performance isn't affected significantly; 1 = level of activity is limited by the illness; 0 = unable to do any strenuous work. (See warning under "Injuries.")
- *Most-recent run:* 3 = went more than fifteen continuous minutes; 2 = completed between ten to fifteen minutes non-stop; 1 = ran between five to ten minutes; 0 = able to run less than five minutes without stopping, or no recent running.
- *Running background:* 3 = have trained for running within the last year; 2 = no running training within the last one to two years; 1 = no running training for more than two years; 0 = have never trained formally for running.
- Related activities: 3 = regularly participate in steady-paced, prolonged activities such as bicycling, hiking, swimming; 2 = regularly practice vigorous "stop-and-go" sports such as tennis, basketball, soccer; 1 = regularly participate in "slow sports" such as golf, baseball, football; 0 = not currently active in any regular sports or exercise programs.
- *Age:* 3 = younger than twenty; 2 = twenty to twenty-nine; 1 = thirty to thirty-nine; 0 = forty or older.
- *Weight:* 3 = at ideal weight; 2 = less than ten pounds above ideal weight; 1 = ten to nineteen pounds above ideal weight; 0 = more than twenty pounds above ideal weight.
- *Resting pulse rate:* 3 = below sixty beats per minute; 2 = sixty to sixty-nine beats; 1 = seventy to seventy-nine beats; 0 = eighty or more beats.
- *Smoking habits:* 3 = never have smoked regularly; 2 = have been a regular smoker but quit; 1 = an occasional smoker; 0 = a regular smoker.

Table 13.1 *Fitness Rating*

Grade yourself according to the standards listed under the heading "Self-Analysis".

Cardiovascular health: _____

Injuries: _____

Illnesses: _____

Most-recent run: _____

Running background: _____

Related activities: _____

Age: _____

Weight: _____

Resting pulse: _____

Smoking habits: _____

Total _____

A total score of twenty or higher indicates excellent fitness for a beginning runner. You probably can handle continuous running for the prescribed periods and may find that the early weeks of the program are too easy for you. Skip ahead if you wish.

A score in the ten to nineteen range is average. You may need to take some walking breaks to complete the assigned runs.

A score of less than ten is below average. You may consider starting with walking only, increasing the sessions to thirty minutes before adding any running.

Extrance Exam

You've approached the starting line by taking a survey of your fitness with pen and paper. Now comes the time for checking it where it counts: on the run.

Kenneth Cooper, the man made the word "aerobics" popular, has conducted extensive tests on beginners with either a twelve-minute or one and one-half-mile run. The Cooper tests rate runners according to how much distance they can cover in that twelve-minute time limit or how fast they can run six laps on a standard outdoor track. He says the results correlate quite closely with those obtained from sophisticated laboratory measurements of fitness.

Table 13.2 First Test

Run one mile and record the time. Grade the run by the standards used in the *Runner's World* National Fun-Run Program. (Warning: Persons with a history of serious medical conditions should not take this test unless they receive medical clearance.)

Grade	Sex	13–19	20–29	30–39	Age 40–49	50–59	60+
A+	Women	7:00	7:30	8:00	8:30	9:00	9:30
	Men	6:00	6:30	7:00	7:30	8:00	8:30
A	Women	7:30	8:00	8:30	9:00	9:30	10:00
	Men	6:30	7:00	7:30	8:00	8:30	9:00
B	Women	8:30	9:00	9:30	10:00	10:30	11:00
	Men	7:30	8:00	8:30	9:00	9:30	10:00
C	Women	9:30	10:00	10:30	11:00	11:30	12:00
	Men	8:30	9:00	9:30	10:00	10:30	11:00
D	Women	11:00	11:30	12:00	12:30	13:00	13:30
	Men	10:00	10:30	11:00	11:30	12:00	12:30
F	Women	11:01+	11:31+	12:01+	12:31+	13:01+	13:31+
	Men	10:01+	10:31+	11:01+	11:31+	12:01+	12:31+

Your age: _____

Your sex: _____

Mile time: _____

Fitness rating: _____

You may want to take a similar, optional test at a slightly shorter distance than Dr. Cooper recommends. Yours is one mile. The reason for the change is more psychological than physical. The physiological reactions to running six and four laps are quite similar, yet the mile is a much more glamorous distance—the most common standard by which runners are measured. Even people who aren't runners know the meaning of mile times.

Test yourself on a track or a carefully measured, flat route. *Don't race* at full speed. Run at a comfortable pace, taking walking breaks if necessary.

Grade yourself by the standards in Table 13.2, but don't take these results too seriously. Personal progress is what you seek, and this test merely draws a baseline from which to improve in tests to follow.

CHAPTER FOURTEEN

The Action

Running Form

How do you run? This isn't a question of how far or how fast or what you do in training, but rather how you move in these directions. How do you put your feet down? How do you look when you run?

You probably haven't thought much about it, and most of the time that's the way to treat this basically automatic action. Running is like breathing. It usually goes along just fine without your thinking about it. Anyway, you can't do much to change the running form you've grown up with, and concentrating too hard on individual steps may throw off the overall flow of the run.

The way you look doesn't matter much, either. This isn't gymnastics of figure skating, and stylish running scores no points. If it did, several Olympic champions would not have won their gold medals. One prominent distance runner, four-time Olympic gold medalist Emil Zatopek, thrashed his arms and grimaced like a crazed street-fighter. Jim Ryun, former world record-holder in the mile, rolled his head from side to side. Sprinter Bob Hayes was so pigeon-toed that he almost stepped on his own feet as he ran. Yet all three were most efficient and effective runners. Their "faults" were no more than innocent personal quirks.

We must be careful when talking about running styles to separate what's wrong from what's merely different. Running doesn't have to look pretty. It only has to feel right for the person doing it. "Right" covers a wide range of individual differences.

Four essential rules apply here:

1. *The form must fit the individual.* A five-foot two-inch runner, for instance, can't use the stride length of someone a foot taller.
2. *The form must fit the pace.* Sprinters can't fall back on their heels without losing speed, while distance runners can't stay up on their toes without getting sore. The form of a runner like you more closely resembles walking than sprinting.
3. *The form must be mechanically efficient.* Man has evolved into an upright animal, and runs best that way: with a straight back.
4. *The form must be relaxed.* Running with tension is like driving a car with its brakes on: you work harder while going slower.

Noted writer on running techniques Ken Doherty advises, "Do what comes naturally, as long as "naturally" is mechnically sound. If it isn't, do what is mechanically sound until it comes naturally."

This chapter deals only with fixing mechanical defects which can and should be corrected.

Heads Up

You've seen this runner. He or she shuffles around the track like a beast of burden—eyes on the feet, back in the shape of a number "9," shoulders hunched, bottom sticking out in back. It looks like gravity is dragging this runner down.

"A forward lean," states retired University of Oregon coach Bill Bowerman, "might be useful for someone trying to bash down a wall. But in running, it merely gives the leg muscles a lot of unnecessary work."

Straighten up, Bowerman advises. "The best postural position for a distance runner is an upright one. A line from the ear straight down to the ground should show the back is perpendicular to the ground while running."

Bowerman says the ideal posture is one in which you could drop a plumbline from ear level, and it would fall "straight down through the line of the shoulder, the line of the hip and then onto the ground."

The advantages are many: freer use of the legs through a greater range of motion; easier breathing as the lungs fill more completely with air; the chance to look at something besides the ground in front of you.

"Run tall!" is an order that track coaches frequently give their athletes. This means stretching up to one's full height, but stopping short of running with the rigid back of a soldier at attention.

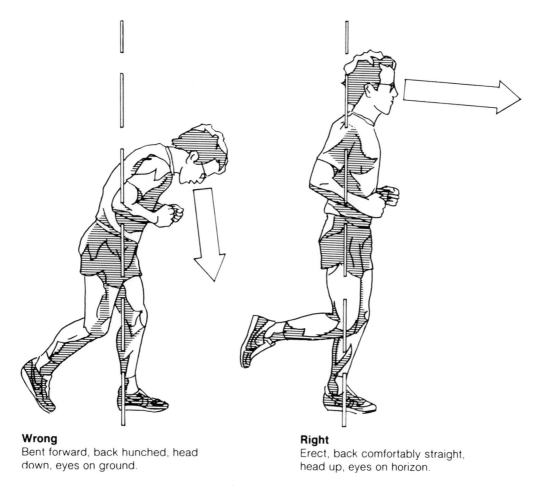

Wrong
Bent forward, back hunched, head
down, eyes on ground.

Right
Erect, back comfortably straight,
head up, eyes on horizon.

Figure 14.1 Running Posture

Good posture begins just above the hips. "The position of the pelvis is the key to postural control in running," says coach Bowerman. "It is a well-known principle of postural correction that forward rotation of the pelvis results in extension of the spine into a sway-backed postion, increased internal rotation of the thighs, secondary lowering of the longitudinal arch, a relative lessening of the ability to flex the hip in relation to the ground, and a forward shift of the center of gravity so that weight falls more heavily on the ball of the foot."

You don't have to understand all the terms to realize that the overall influence of a pelvic tilt isn't good for runners. Regard the pelvis as a filled bowl, and try not to spill its contents by with a forward lean.

The other key to postural control is the head. The gaze of the eyes controls the lean of the body. Look down, and you'll run like a "9." Cast your eyes on the horizon, parallel to the ground, and everything else tends to fall into proper alignment.

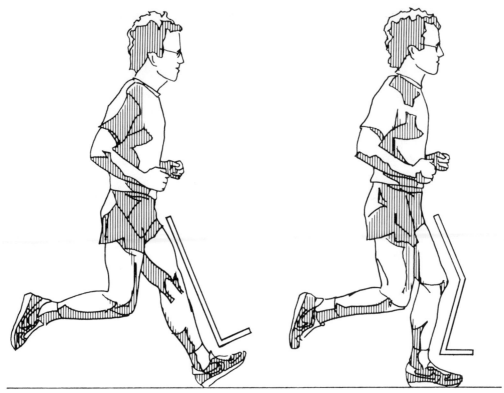

Wrong
Landing heel-first, knee straightened, ankle locked.

Right
Landing on midfoot, knee slightly flexed, ankle unlocked.

Figure 14.2 Running Footplant

Feet First

Some runners will never sneak up behind you. Even without looking over your shoulder, you can hear them coming: *Clomp! Clomp! Clomp!* You can almost feel the impact shock.

The noise indicates two related problems: overstriding (reaching out too far with the feet) and landing with the knee locked. These faults cause the runner to plant the foot heel first, then to slap down on the forefoot as the ankle unlocks. The result: the foot and leg act more like as crutch than the shock-absorber they're meant to be.

In proper footplant, the knee is slightly flexed so that it can bend on impact. This causes the foot to land more directly under the body and at midfoot rather than heel-first. As the ankle unlocks, you rock back onto the heel, then forward again for lift-off. The overall result is a more silent brand of running.

Runners fall into two general categories: those who run *on* the ground and try to pound it flat, and those who run *off* the ground, using the earth as a springboard for staying airborne. The latter should serve as your model.

In making your running more springy, check the foot, ankle, and knee.

- *Foot.* Make full use of it, from midfoot to heel to toes, as you roll through the running motion. Give a little push with the big toe as you leave the ground.
- *Ankle.* Flex it. Use it to get more bounce. The more rigid the ankle is, the more jarring the contact with the ground will be.
- *Knee.* Lift it. The lift of the knee controls the fall of the foot. If the knee rides low and rigid, you feet will barely clear the ground. Pick up the knee and bend it.
- *Prance.* Keep this one word in mind as you perfect your foot-leg action. Run as if you're proud of yourself—silently proud, that is.

The Arms' Place

You know both types of runners. The first runs like a boxer trying to protect the face; the arms ride high and tight, and the fists stop just short of the chin. The opposite type of runner holds the arms straight down to the sides with fingers pointed at the ground, as if these appendages served no useful purpose. Neither runner's arms do much good.

In fact, they shouldn't just be along for the ride. The hands and arms fill important roles in two-legged locomotion. The hands control tension, as you can easily demonstrate to yourself. Hold out your hand, straighten the fingers, and notice the feeling of rigidity all the way up the arm. Now make a fist and clench it tightly. You're tense again, right? Finally, make a loose fist. Feel better? The unclenched fist, fingers resting lightly on the palms, promotes relaxed running.

Move up the arm, and check the wrist. It should be fixed in line with the arm, not flapping aimlessly in the breeze. If nothing else, this looks sloppy.

Give careful attention to the elbow. It should always be unlocked. Otherwise, you sacrifice the driving and balancing potential of the arms. The arms get their power from the up-and-down motion at elbow level. Try hammering a nail with a stiff elbow, then take advantage of the bend and notice the superiority of the second method. Similar forces are at work in running.

The locked elbow also produces one of the most common form faults: dipping and swaying shoulders, a most wasteful motion. Ideally, the shoulders show no apparent movement. They remain parallel to the running surface.

The arms swing in rhythm with the legs. The faster the beat, the more violently the arms move. This accounts for the piston-like drive of sprinters. The action is more pendulum-like in distance running. The range of motion is smaller, and the arms swing somewhat across the chest—but not past the midline.

In summary, run with loose fists, fixed wrists, flexible elbows, and shoulders so level you could carry chips on them.

Wrong
Arms too high and tight, hands held at upper chest level

Wrong
Arms dangling at sides, fingers extended

Right
Arms swinging between waistband and lower chest, elbows unlocked

Figure 14.3 Running Arm Action

The Additions

Extra Exercise

"When a runner goes into training," says George Sheehan, M.D., "three things can happen to the muscles. Two of them are bad: shortening of the strengthened muscles with loss of flexibility; weakness of the opposing, relative unused muscles."

This doesn't happen all at once. You probably won't experience either of these problems until you are an experienced runner. The effects are cumulative, with runners becoming increasingly tight and out of muscular balance unless corrective action is taken.

Running, by itself, isn't enough—not if you want to be all-around fit. Some leg muscles grow super-strong, while opposing ones are allowed to be lazy. The arms, shoulders, chest, back, and abdominal muscles don't get much of a workout.

Ironically, some of the most highly conditioned distance runners are less likely than non-athletes to pass simple tests of strength and flexibility: lifting a large portion of the body weight, doing a number of situps, bending over and touching the fingertips to the floor without bending the knees.

Exercises such as pushups and bent-leg situps can restore and maintain much of the upper-body strength lost through specialization and neglect. Another type of balance is more critical because it affects health. As mentioned, the front-of-leg muscles don't develop during running as back-of-leg muscles do. Pains in the shins and knees may set in.

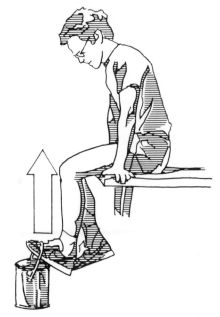

Upper-leg exercise. Sit on a table with a light weight (such as a paint can) hanging from foot. Extend leg from the knee 20 or more times. Repeat with other leg.

Lower-leg exercise. Sit on a table with the light weight hanging from one foot. Flex the ankle 20 or more times. Repeat with other ankle.

Figure 15.1 Leg Strengthening

A simple way to strengthen these muscles is to sit on a table with your legs dangling, hang a weight on one foot, and straighten the leg repeatedly (see Figure 15.1). This helps the muscles from the knee up. For the lower leg, flex the ankle up and down. Bicycling yields many of these same benefits.

Lack of flexibility is a notable problem for runners who've trained a long time. The sport tightens them, exposing them to muscle and tendon strains that might not have happened if they had remained supple.

A great advance in recent years has been the growing popularity of so-called "static" stretching exercises. These involve moving slowly to a position at the point of discomfort, then holding that position for a period. These stretches differ from traditional calisthenics both in style and effect. The movements in calisthenics are violent, and they can actually exaggerate the tightening they are supposed to prevent. Static stretching gently loosens the muscles.

Figures 15.2 through 15.6 illustrate a quick but effective five-minute exercise program (including pushups for strength) that you can do without having to flop down on the cold, wet, or lumpy ground. Remember to keep all stretches *slow,* to hold the final position for at least ten seconds, and to stay out of the pain zone.

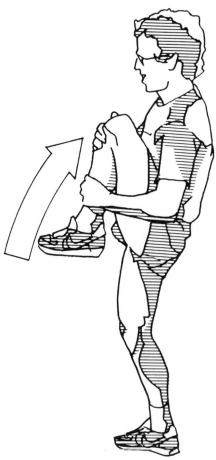

Part one: Cradle a lower leg and pull it toward chest.

Figure 15.2 The Leg Puller

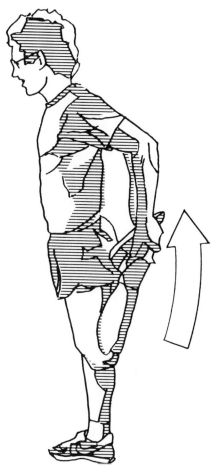

Part two: Grasp a foot behind back, and pull toward buttocks. Repeat parts one and two with other leg.

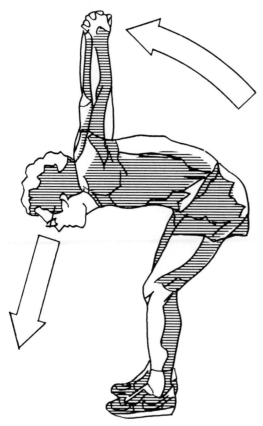

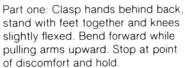

Part one: Clasp hands behind back, stand with feet together and knees slightly flexed. Bend forward while pulling arms upward. Stop at point of discomfort and hold.

Part two: Drop arms until palms touch ground in front of feet. The less flexible you are, the farther in front of the toes you will touch.

Figure 15.3 The Toe Touch

Part one: Stand with legs spread. Turn one foot outward, then bend in that direction.

Part two: Turn in the direction of bend, step forward, and reach as far ahead as possible. Repeat parts one and two on the other side.

Figure 15.4 The Triangle

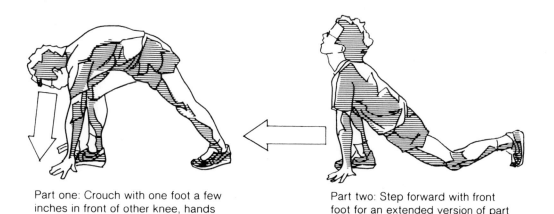

Part one: Crouch with one foot a few inches in front of other knee, hands on ground. Then straighten rear leg.

Part two: Step forward with front foot for an extended version of part one. Repeat both exercises with opposite foot forward.

Figure 15.5 The Sprinter

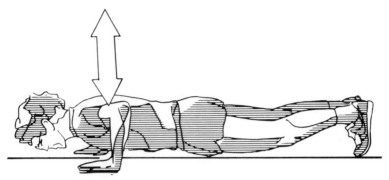

Standard pushup. From straight-armed starting position, touch nose, chest, and upper legs to floor, keeping back straight. Work up to 20 or more repetitions.

Figure 15.6 The Pushup

Exercise Alternatives

Not everyone is meant to be a lifelong, full-time runner, and there is no need to be one. Mixing and matching sports can produce similar results—as long as the exercises are aerobic and they're applied regularly for adequate time periods. Kenneth Cooper, M.D., says, "The best exercises are running, swimming, cycling, walking, stationary running, handball, basketball, and squash—in just about that order."

The body requires continuous activity, but it isn't too particular about the type. Running is the quickest way to reach the quota of aerobic exercise recommended by Dr. Cooper. But there are other good approaches to the same goal.

Cooper's minimum standard for fitness is thirty aerobic points a week. A mile in eight minutes counts for five of these points, and six of those miles equal thirty points weekly. (For reference, a six-minute mile gains you six points, and a ten-minute mile three points.)

The approximate equivalents of an eight-minute mile for other exercises are listed here.

- Swimming 600 yards in fifteen minutes
- Bicycling five miles in twenty minutes
- Walking three miles in forty minutes
- Running in place for twelve and one-half minutes
- Handball for thirty-five minutes

A runner with a slight injury, too tender to stand much pounding but not serious enough for crutches, might bicycle his or her points. Another might substitute swimming on a humid, ninety-degree afternoon. Cross-country skiing isn't included on Dr. Cooper's list, but apparently its aerobic effects are almost identical to running's—and gliding across the snow is more pleasant than plowing through it.

P A R T   S I X

THE RUNNING BASICS

*I*f writers can be divided into two groups—those who praise their subjects too highly and those who knock them too hard—I'm a praiser. We praisers have been guilty of exaggerating the arguments for running, of seeming to say that once you get into shape, running is easy . . . except when you race, and then you risk running into a "wall." We seem to assert that running immunizes you against all the diseases of sedentary humankind; that this is a drugless "high"; a "religion" with its own gospels, saints, rituals, and places of worship.

I've praised running too much at times. Now I write from a place between the two extremes. If I "de-mystify" running a little bit, maybe runners can more easily find what they want in it, and non-runners can better judge what it is.

- *The fun.* Running isn't fun all the time, and it never is fun for very long. Parts of each day's run—and often whole runs—are no fun at all. You work through the bad spells because a couple of miles a day, or a day or two a week, are really satisfying. These moments make up for the trouble of getting to them.
- *The ease.* Running isn't easy for anyone past puberty, and the kind of running that many of us do (long, steady, and on hard surfaces) isn't easy or natural even for children. We only make it comfortable the way all other athletes do: by training to learn a specialized skill which isn't much like the running we did on the playground as kids. We need specific instruction in how to run in this fashion.

- *The pain.* Runners face different types and degrees of pain. Good pains warn us away from trouble before we hurt ourselves too much. Bad ones come when we ignore the good and can't run as a result. Blisters, sore muscles, labored breathing, and temporary fatigue are not reasons to run or to stop running; they are simply by-products of running. The "wall" marathoners talk about is nothing more awesome than a warning against training too little or starting too fast.
- *The health.* I'm slow to cite medical evidence either about the miracles running works on the body or the damage it causes. No other sport—from skiing to football—is praised or condemned as much for its physical results. Talking of running in medical terms makes it seem more a form of therapy or torture than what it is at its best: a sport.
- *The "high."* I prefer to think of running not as a natural high but as a natural laxative. It throws off the wastes clogging the body and mind. This usually takes about thirty minutes. After that, the way is clear for smooth running and good thinking. Instead of this being a mystical experience, I think of it as the way we're supposed to feel when not constipated.
- *The "religion."* Both religion and running involve making sacrifices now for greater joy later. But this is where their similarity ends. In fact, the two are more opposite than alike. Religion implies belief in a force bigger and better than any person can be. Running is indulgence of the self and what it can become.

We need to praise running only for what it is. There are safer ways to exercise than this, better ways to cure diseases, quicker ways to get high, truer ways to find religion, easier ways to have fun. I don't deny that running gives some of these things. But praising them too highly hides what we really have here: a sport which, like all sports, offers both pain and joy, both risk and reward.

We praise running enough just by saying there is no finer sport than this. Personal measures of time and distance give anyone a chance to win.

The Buildup

Sources of the System

The names Bill Bowerman, Kenneth Cooper, M.D., and Arthur Lydiard loom largest in what has come to be called the "running boom." They made it possible for running to be more than a sport for elite young athletes by changing the training techniques and attitudes that dominated running in the past.

Bowerman was a renowned track coach at the University of Oregon. He traveled to New Zealand in the early 1960s and met Lydiard, an even more prominent coach. Bowerman was most impressed by the thousands of New Zealanders of all ages and abilities whom Lydiard had introduced to running. Bowerman began to run himself when he returned home, and thousands of Americans soon followed his lead.

Lydiard, a one-time marathon runner and coach of several Olympic champions, abandoned the track-oriented training methods of his era in favor of extensive distance running on the roads. He then translated this system into schedules that beginning runners could use.

Dr. Cooper adapted the ideas of Bowerman and Lydiard by carrying them several steps further. While serving in the Air Force, he tested hundreds of thousands of military personnel for their reactions to exercise. He concluded that aerobic-type activity was most beneficial and that running was the most efficient of these exercises. His book *Aerobics,* first published in 1968 and updated several times since, won millions of converts to running.

Your build-up program (see Table 16.1) is largely a synthesis of Cooper-Lydiard-Bowerman ideas which revolutionized this activity. The vital points are presented here.

- Cover at least ten to fifteen minutes. According to Cooper, it takes about ten minutes of continuous movement before any training benefit is achieved. The three experts agree that this is bare-minimum running time, so you start at this level and work up.
- Use the "talk test." This term is Bowerman's. He says if you can talk while you run, you're doing fine. If you're gasping, you're going too fast. (A more complicated but also more exact alternative is pulse-rate monitoring. See the "How Fast?" section of this chapter.)
- "Train, don't strain." This is Lydiard's catch-phrase. Running should *not* be exhausting, particularly at this early stage. Lydiard says you should rarely go beyond the limits of "pleasant tiredness."
- Run by time. Lydiard encourages beginners to concern themselves only with time periods, not with distances. You can rush a mile or two in order to finish sooner. But time can't be hurried along, so you're more likely to run your minutes at a comfortable, safe pace.
- Employ "intervals" if necessary. This is another Bowerman tip: Start the ten- to fifteen-minute period with the intention of running as much of it as you can, remembering to keep it aerobic and unstrained. If breathing becomes labored or pains set in, slow to a walk until you feel recovered, then resume running. Repeat as required.
- Challenge yourself occasionally. All three experts are former competitors who recognize the motivational values of racing. They all build tests of one form or another into their programs to add excitement. You are encourged to progress toward testing yourself in longer and faster-than-normal runs and races.

How Far?

Run long enough but not too long. Long enough to get most of the physical benefits isn't very long. Most experts agree that these gains can be accomplished with fifteen- to thirty-minute runs. You certainly can keep your body reasonably fit on a couple of miles a day a few days a week.

However, one doctor notes that the body also has a head attached, and the mind has different requirements. Psychiatrist Thaddeus Kostrubala is as much a pioneer as Dr. Cooper, having used running as a therapeutic tool for a decade. Dr. Kostrubala says his patients feel terrible early in their runs, but if he nurses them through these doldrums and takes them to thirty minutes or more, their symptoms improve. The most productive therapy sessions follow the longer runs.

Normal runners experience this same pattern. The early minutes aren't often pleasant, even for fit athletes who have run for years. This is a time for warming up and for finding the running rhythm. Runners wade through the first mile or two so they can get to the good part, which may not arrive until until a half-hour has passed.

Table 16.1 A New Beginning

The first goal of new runners (as well as those returning from lapses of activity) should be to establish a daily exercise habit. That's why this program recommends six-day running weeks, and a seventh day when a run is optional. The second goal is to work toward a half-hour daily average. The third goal: working up to an hour on the week's long run. If you now are running less than these amounts, enter this program one step up from current level. For instance, if you're averaging twenty minutes (total time divided by seven, even if not running every day), begin in fifth week. Run at a pace that allows you to finish these runs comfortably. Record your actual runs by day and your averages by week. If a week seems unusually difficult, repeat it or back down one step.

First Week (Average: 13 Minutes)

Day	Suggested Run	Actual Run
1	15 minutes	_____
2	15 minutes	_____
3	15 minutes	_____
4	15 minutes	_____
5	15 minutes	_____
6	20 minutes	_____
7	Optional	_____
	Daily Average:	_____

Second Week (Average: 15 Minutes)

Day	Suggested Run	Actual Run
1	15 minutes	_____
2	15 minutes	_____
3	15 minutes	_____
4	15 minutes	_____
5	15 minutes	_____
6	30 minutes	_____
7	Optional	_____
	Daily Average:	_____

Third Week (Average: 18 Minutes)

Day	Suggested Run	Actual Run
1	20 minutes	_____
2	20 minutes	_____
3	20 minutes	_____
4	20 minutes	_____
5	20 minutes	_____
6	30 minutes	_____
7	Optional	_____
	Daily Average:	_____

Fourth Week (Average: 20 Minutes)

Day	Suggested Run	Actual Run
1	20 minutes	_____
2	20 minutes	_____
3	20 minutes	_____
4	20 minutes	_____
5	20 minutes	_____
6	40 minutes	_____
7	Optional	_____
	Daily Average:	_____

Table 16.1—*Continued*

Fifth Week (Average: 23 Minutes)

Day	Suggested Run	Actual Run
1	25 minutes	_____
2	25 minutes	_____
3	25 minutes	_____
4	25 minutes	_____
5	25 minutes	_____
6	40 minutes	_____
7	Optional	_____
	Daily Average:	_____

Sixth Week (Average: 25 Minutes)

Day	Suggested Run	Actual Run
1	25 minutes	_____
2	25 minutes	_____
3	25 minutes	_____
4	25 minutes	_____
5	25 minutes	_____
6	50 minutes	_____
7	Optional	_____
	Daily Average:	_____

Seventh Week (Average: 28 Minutes)

Day	Suggested Run	Actual Run
1	30 minutes	_____
2	30 minutes	_____
3	30 minutes	_____
4	30 minutes	_____
5	30 minutes	_____
6	50 minutes	_____
7	Optional	_____
	Daily Average:	_____

Eighth Week (Average: 30 Minutes)

Day	Suggested Run	Actual Run
1	30 minutes	_____
2	30 minutes	_____
3	30 minutes	_____
4	30 minutes	_____
5	30 minutes	_____
6	60 minutes	_____
7	Optional	_____
	Daily Average:	_____

For this reason, you're asked to fit your run into at least a thirty-minute period right from the start. You do this as much for the head as the heart, because the longer exercise periods are more satisfying. Walking occupies more than half of the time at first, but you should work toward a goal of running comfortably for an uninterrupted half-hour or more.

Experienced runners typically stay in the thirty- to sixty-minute time frame. This is long enough to be rewarding but short enough to remain good, healthy fun; long enough to make you want to come back for more but short enough to allow you to do so. Runs in this range fill the pool of enthusiasm without draining the energy pool.

How Fast?

Run slowly, but not *too* slowly. George Sheehan, M.D., who ranks close to Dr. Cooper as a promoter of running, cautions, "If the pace is too slow, it does very little good. On the other hand, a too-fast pace is self-defeating."

"Comfortable" is the key word, according to Dr. Sheehan. He tells runners to "set your inner dial just below the discomfort zone, then stay there—easing off the pace whenever it starts to hurt or increasing it when it feels too easy." Sheehan insists that the body knows—much more precisely than any stopwatch or training schedule can tell it—what proper pace is.

The trick is to cooperate with pain as a friend instead of fighting it as an enemy. This ties in with the concept known in yoga as "playing the edge." Ian Jackson, who did almost as much to popularize yoga-like exercises for runners as Drs. Cooper and Sheehan did for running, says you should run the same way you stretch.

Jackson recommends stretching carefully to the point of discomfort, backing off slightly, then holding that "edge" for a few seconds. The first thing you notice is that the edge moves farther out without any excess strain. You notice, after a few weeks of stretching this way, that the edge of comfort has moved to a point you earlier could only reach with great pain.

Playing the edge also applies to the pace at which you run. It means finding that invisible line between comfort and discomfort. If you never nudge it, you never move it farther out—but if you push too hard, it breaks you.

If you want a more precise measurement, check your pulse immediately after stopping a run. Proper aerobic pace corresponds to approximately seventy-five percent of your maximum pulse rate. This top figure is rather difficult to determine, so Samuel Fox, M.D., former president of the American College of Cardiology, devised a rule of thumb: he simply subtracts age from 170. A forty-year-old, then, should treat 130 as his or her peak exercising pulse rate.

As you advance in running, you'll learn to apply numbers to comfortable pacing. Later, you'll know what your absolute fastest pace is for a short-distance race. A good rule of thumb then will be to train one to two minutes *per mile* slower than that time. A seven-minute-per-mile racer, for instance, would do most of his or her running at eight- to nine-minute pace. This will be slow enough, but not too slow; on the edge, but not over it—the proper gear for most conditions.

How Often?

You should run at least every other day, but not *every* day, in the early stages. There's general agreement among the authorities on this point. It is important to give the body a day or more off each week to deal with the new demands being placed upon it.

Bill Bowerman values rest for all runners. "The well-conditioned runner learns early," he says, "that rest is as important to his or her success as exercise."

Bowerman's major gift to training theory is the "hard-easy" system. Under it, his competing athletes take a hard workout one day, then ease off the next two or three before hitting another hard day.

"In thirty years of training national- and international-class runners," asserts Bowerman, "I have found that they progress more rapidly and painlessly by an alternating program of hard-easy. Chronic fatigue states are avoided."

The experts agree on three days a week as a minimum requirement for fitness. They agree, too, that you need at least one day of rest during the initial build-up. The program in Table 16.1 is true to those recommendations while it attempts to make exercising an everyday habit. In keeping with Bowerman's "hard-easy" advice, most of the runs are relatively brief, and one run each week is longer than the others.

The Racing

At the Races

The longest stride a runner ever takes, you've already taken. That was the first one out the door on your first run. A runner's second-longest step is the one you might be thinking of taking, the one that would put you on the starting line of your first race.

The thought alternately intrigues and intimidates you. You've been running for a while, and you've graduated from the first trudges around the block to comfortable half-hour runs. You're looking for a new challenge. You watched the big local 10-K last year, and you think, "Maybe I could. . . ."

Then the dream gives way to doubts: "What if I finish last? What if I can't finish at all? What if I look silly in front of my friends and neighbors?" You put the thought of racing aside, but it keeps coming back.

Should you race? Only if you are convinced that you'll be a more complete runner with racing than you are without it. If you enjoy running for the solitude it offers, and if you feel no urge to increase distances or improve times, racing has little to offer you. If you yearn to mix with other runners both as companions and competitors, however, and if you're hungry to test your mileage and speed limits, you're ready to go public with your running. Fill out a race entry blank.

Perhaps all entry forms should carry a warning: "Caution—this event may be hazardous to your health." That would tell you what you're getting into and why. Racing is hard work, and that effort can hurt you. It contributes little or nothing to fitness, and may even detract from it by increasing fatigue and the risk of injury. However, racing does offer an incentive to stick with everyday runs—which do add to fitness.

Author Tom Osler calls racing an "indirect benefit." He muses, "I can't imagine one of my 800-plus races that did my health any good. Racing is simply too hard to be placed in the healthful-exercise category. Yet if it were not for my interest in racing, I probably would have abandoned my training runs long ago. These runs have been an enormous boon to my general well-being, both physical and mental."

Try one race. Otherwise, you'll never know whether racing attracts or repels you. More often than not, runners get caught up in the excitement of these events.

Modern mass-participation road races can be fun if approached in the spirit that dominates these occasions. The idea is not to cross the finish line first, but to "win" on your own terms. That may simply mean completing the course, running farther than you ever have before, or holding a faster pace.

Those of you who have never raced before will find it easiest to win. You'll find it almost impossible to finish last, which is the great fear of beginners. No matter how slow you are, there'll always be someone slower because you now have done your homework and many other entrants have not.

Three recommendations for first-timer racers:

- *Select your event carefully.* Find a race that won't embarrass or discourage you, at a distance you're capable of finishing. You'll fit most comfortably into a large road race of about ten kilometers.
- *Be prepared.* Run this full distance at least once by yourself before putting yourself on the racing line. A ten-kilometer racer, for instance, should be taking long runs in the one-hour range.
- *Pace yourself.* Resist getting caught up in the opening rush and starting too fast. The most efficient pace is one that holds steady for the entire distance.

Race Types

Road races are the best thing that ever happened to this sport. Not long ago, the only way one could run a race was to be young and fast. The only types of racing available were track and cross-country, and these usually were limited to elite male athletes who were high school or college students.

That all changed in the 1970s. Road racing grew from a small stepchild of track and field to being the dominant branch of the sport. While track and cross-country still are sports for the select few (the only notable change is the new role of women), the roads grow increasingly crowded. The Bay to Breakers race in San Francisco draws more than 50,000 runners annually; the Bloomsday run in Spokane and the Peachtree event in Atlanta attract more than 25,000 each, and races throughout the country host casts of thousands every weekend of the year.

Several factors explain this popularity. One is the training trend of the last twenty years, when long-distance running has come into style. Athletes preparing for standard track and cross-country competition turned to the long road training to make themselves stronger, then found they liked the roads enough to want to race there. Meanwhile, thousands of people began running distances for fitness, and as they grew fit they looked for new challenges at the races.

These roads had plenty of room for all types, and they all came to recognize that these races offered the most democratic arena in the sports world. Runners of every age, ability, and ambition joined together at common starting lines. Lining up at the Boston or New York Marathons was the average runner's equivalent of playing in the U.S. Open or driving the Indianapolis 500.

There are road races for every taste: big ones, small ones; short ones, long ones; hilly ones, flat ones. Generally speaking, the distances fit into categories: short (requiring no more than an hour to run), medium (one to two hours), long (two hours-plus), and ultra-long (beyond the marathon distance of 26.22 miles). Table 17.1 lists the standard racing events and translates metric distances to miles.

As a new racer, you're wise to stick with the short events. Hold the marathon in your dreams for now.

Race Training

The goal of a first-time racer is to reach the finish line with a proud smile on his or her face. This may surprise you, but you're already prepared to finish a short road race.

The program in Chapter 16 (Table 16.1) led to weekly long runs of an hour, or about ten kilometers. Even relatively inexperienced runners cover that much ground in an hour's time. And that happens to be the most popular racing distance.

Once you have passed the one-hour test with non-stop running, you can safely enter a race with no further special preparation. Only if you want to race farther and faster does the program require any modifications, and these are only slight.

Training for improved racing is no great mystery. The essential ingredients are (1) some runs of full racing distance but at a slower pace, and (2) some runs of full racing speed but at a shorter distance. These grow longer and faster as the demands of racing do. You only combine the elements—full distance and full speed—in actual races.

Only one run a week is affected: the one big day of either testing or racing. The other days remain just about as they are now. Half-hour runs are long enough to maintain your conditioning, short enough to let you relax between the harder efforts. A rest day each week is not only allowed but encouraged. You're putting harsher demands on yourself, and you need these recovery breaks. (Part Eight covers advanced training techniques in more detail.)

Table 17.1 *Racing Distances*

Almost all races are now run under the metric system, so runners must learn the meaning of distances in kilometers. Listed here are the standard events and their mile equivalents. One kilometer is 1000 meters or sixty-two hundredths of a mile. A marathon isn't an even distance in either system; it extends 26.22 miles or 42.19 kilometers.

Metric	Mile
1500 meters	.93 mile
3 kilometers	1.86 miles
5 kilometers	3.11 miles
8 kilometers	4.97 miles
10 kilometers	6.21 miles
12 kilometers	7.46 miles
15 kilometers	9.32 miles
20 kilometers	12.43 miles
25 kilometers	15.54 miles
30 kilometers	18.64 miles
50 kilometers	31.08 miles

Race Tactics

Survival. That is the only tactic that need concern you as a novice in this game. Surviving comes from equal parts of preparation and restraint.

Runners talk in hushed tones about the prospects of "hitting the wall" in a race. They act as if this feeling of suddenly dragging an anchor or carrying a bear on their back is an inevitable part of racing. It is not. Hitting the wall is a mistake of either training inadequately or pacing improperly.

We've talked about training requirements. Based on your work record, finishing a 10-K should only be a matter of keeping your wits about you. That, of course, is easier written than accomplished.

Table 17.2 *First-Race Survival*

1. Choose a big road race—the bigger the better. That way, you'll be assured of having the company of hundreds of first-timers just like yourself. The excitement of that crowd will carry you along.

2. Avoid track or cross-country races. These are small and serious, and the experience of running alone and over your head might turn you away from racing forever.

3. Be part of this race, but don't *race* it. In other words, run to finish this first time, at your normal long-test pace or only slightly faster.

4. Run no farther than you have gone in training. Your peak in this program is one hour, or roughly ten kilometers, so choose this popular 6.2-mile distance or a shorter one.

5. Do nothing new on raceday. Wear the shoes and clothes that you know are comfortable, and eat (or don't eat) as you would before any other run.

6. Go to the race with an experienced advisor. This sport is all new and a little frightening, and someone who has been here at least once before can steady you.

7. Start in the middle of the pack or farther back. The serious folks line up in the front and race away from the line very quickly, trampling anyone who gets in their way.

8. Start slowly (in fact, you'll have little choice in a crowded race). Let the overeager people sprint away. Many of them will come back to you later, and it's much more fun to pass than to be passed.

9. Time yourself, since "official" times at these races are notoriously inaccurate. Start your watch as you cross the starting line, not when the gun sounds. The seconds or even minutes spent shuffling to the line shouldn't be lost.

10. Be nice. Some jostling is inevitable in the big races, but the etiquette of the sport frowns upon zig-zagging wildly through the human traffic, cutting sharply in front of runners, or elbowing your way to a better position.

Even if you've done everything right in training, you can cancel all that good with as little as one wrong move on raceday. The first and worst bad move is leaving the starting line too quickly. Crowd hysteria and your own raging nervous system conspire to send you into the race as if fired from a cannon.

Particularly in your first race, try to work against the forces of the crowd and your natural desires. Keep your head while those around you are losing theirs. Pull back the mental reins at a time when the voices inside are shouting, "Faster, faster!" Be extremely cautious in your early pacing, erring on the side of "too slow" rather than "too fast." Hold something in reserve for the late kilometers.

The time for going to the whip is after halfway point. Then, the time for restraint has passed, and you run the rest of the way with whatever energy you have left. Again, you stand apart from the crowd. You hold your pace while others are losing control of theirs. This is where you reward yourself for your early caution.

You check your watch at the midpoint, and then again at the finish. You're pleased with the overall result. Likely as not, it is significantly faster than you ever ran by yourself; the adrenaline stirred up by racing has that effect.

Later, you compare your first- and second-half "splits." If the first was considerably faster, plan to start even more conservatively next time. If the second part was vastly superior, feel free to loosen the reins next time.

A steady pace breaks records, while uneven pacing breaks hearts.

CHAPTER EIGHTEEN

The Choices

Just the Beginning

You have just begun to run. You've served your apprenticeship as a runner during the weeks of basic training. Now the choice is yours. Do you want to stop, back down to a lighter running program, continue with what you're doing, test yourself more stringently in competition, or run for emotional therapy?

If you keep running, you'll approach running one of three ways: as a jogger, a racer, or a fun-runner. None of the terms is precise, and the lines between them aren't clearly drawn. For simplicity's sake, though, we can say that a jogger exercises for fitness, a racer trains for competition, and a fun-runner runs purely to be running.

Running interests evolve, both in the individual runner and in the activity as a whole. Typically, the first concern is to become fit, then to push distances and paces to their limits, and finally to treat running as an end in itself. Running as a social phenomenon has passed through similar stages.

The so-called "running boom" had its initial rumblings in the late 1960s when Kenneth Cooper, M.D., wrote his first *Aerobics* book, which promoted running for fitness. More and more people began running, until this became a full-blown fad in the late 1970s. The wave of new runners crested in those years, but that didn't mean everyone suddenly abandoned this activity.

The new runners of the 1970s became the new *racers* of 1980s as their abilities and interests changed. They evolved from jogging short distances alone, to running farther with groups, to entering 10-Ks, to finishing marathons, to racing 10-Ks faster.

A few years later, running continues to mature. This is not to say that no new runners are beginning (you're proof that they are), or that the old ones don't care about fitness anymore, or that racing has lost all of its appeal. It means that thousands of longtime runners have moved to the third stage, where running is more than fitness, less than fanaticism.

In Stage One, you stay adequately fit. In Stage Two, you grow surprisingly fast and enduring. In Stage Three, you still stay in better shape than those who run just for exercise. You still can race as well as many people who train just to race. You still can have the benefits of the two earlier stages, but you don't *need* them as much as you once did.

You don't leave the two earlier stages behind as you evolve toward the third. You simply modify them to fit into your new view. You do more running than the half-hour three or four days a week needed to maintain fitness. But you do less than the fifty-mile weeks—with long runs on weekends and hard speedwork in midweek—needed to set records. The promise of a leaner body and stronger heart or of faster racing times become nice by-products of running instead of main reasons to run.

Running for Fitness

Kenneth Cooper, the man generally credited with putting America on the road to aerobic fitness, is not a fanatical runner. Although he ran in high school and college, and has exercised this way for the last twenty years, he claims he doesn't even particularly like to run. But he likes the results it gives him for a limited time investment. Cooper's typical run lasts less than twenty minutes, and he has mountains of data to prove that this is enough to maintain physical fitness.

Health is the absence of disease or disability; fitness is much more. It is a learned capacity to do work smoothly, efficiently, and with energy to spare. Health is a passive state, while gaining and maintaining fitness is an active process. You can't sit and wait for it to come. You have to chase it by prodding, challenging, stretching yourself. You have to keep running, as Lewis Carroll wrote in *Alice in Wonderland,* just to stay where you are. To make further gains, you need to run even more.

Fortunately, staying fit doesn't require great amounts of running. Dr. Cooper says as little as fifteen to twenty minutes several days a week is adequate. I have called, in the last few chapters, for an increase to a half-hour. If fitness is your only goal, you never need to climb above the thirty-minute figure again.

If you share Cooper's mixed feelings about running, you might settle into a long-term program with these features.

- Run between fifteen and thirty minutes on three weekdays. Make these runs the basis of your fitness program, since they give good results quickly.
- Drop long or fast racing and race-like training from your routine. They contribute nothing to fitness.

- Replace a hard weekend run with another vigorous activity—either aerobic (in the form of bicycling, swimming, cross-country skiing, backpacking, or rowing), or stop-and-go sports such as tennis, racquetball, soccer, and basketball. Regular running provides an endurance base which makes your more enjoyable sports move easier and last longer.

Running for Sport

Joan Ullyot, M.D., wrote the best-seller, *Women's Running.* But before she wrote it, she had to live out the lessons she would pass on to other women. Dr. Ullyot didn't run until she was thirty. She began then for familiar reasons: to lose weight and to rid herself of the lingering effects of a smoking habit.

A few years after struggling to complete a single lap of the track, Ullyot improved enough to compete in the World Marathon Championships. Now in her forties, she still races alongside the top women in her age group.

Trained as a pathologist, Dr. Ullyot switched her specialty to exercise physiology after she became a runner. She carefully monitors the effects of training and racing in both herself and her patients, as she and they perform the tightrope act of running enough to improve but not so much that they break down.

The doctor has devised a set of guidelines to control these stresses. She calls them the "Rules of Ten."

1. "Increase mileage by no more than ten percent per week." A runner at the thirty-mile level last week, for instance, would go no more than thirty-three this week.
2. "No more than one mile in ten as speedwork." A thirty-mile-a-week runner would average no more than five miles of high-speed running, taken either as training or racing.
3. "You won't reach your full potential as an athlete until you have trained for at least ten years." I'd give a slightly lower number, but the point remains. The runner adapts slowly and steadily to the stresses of racing, and improvement continues for years on even modest amounts of training.

If you're serious about racing well for a long time, consider these changes in your program:

- Add two more runs to the weekly schedule, bringing the total to six. You're still wise to allow one rest day a week as recovery from race-like efforts.
- Run at least thirty minutes and not more than an hour as your basic sessions.
- Race regularly at a wide range of distances, or test yourself with longer distances or faster paces almost weekly when true races aren't available.

Running for Life

George Sheehan, M.D., provides the most eloquent one-paragraph description of fun-runners: "For every runner who tours the world running marathons, there are thousands who run to hear the leaves and listen to the rain, and look to the day when it is suddenly as easy as a bird in flight. For them, sport is not a test but a therapy, not a trial but a reward, not a question but an answer."

At one time, Derek Clayton looked like the least possible candidate for this definition. He toured the marathoning world in the sixties and early seventies, running this distance faster than anyone before him. He also trained harder than any marathoner ever has; maybe that's why his world record lasted more than twelve years.

When he trained to a peak, Clayton ran up to 200 miles a week—almost always at racing pace. The reward for this routine was a world record. But there was also a toll to pay. His price was nine surgical operations: from back to knee to Achilles tendon. Enduring all of this pain, day after week after month, simply wore down Clayton's soft tissues.

On retiring from competition, Clayton made this blunt and revealing statement: "I can honestly admit now that I've never enjoyed a single minute of my running, and I'm relieved to be finished with it."

At his last finish line, all that pain hadn't equaled gain. It had added up to more and more pain, until finally it had eroded his health and enthusiasm to the point where he saw no need to fight the pain any more.

But the story doesn't end there. Clayton's racing-induced injuries healed with time. He began missing running a few months after he had "retired" in bitterness and pain. He didn't miss the 200-mile weeks and the marathons that had beaten him down so badly. He missed something about the daily routine of running itself.

Clayton began to run again. This time, he limited himself to a half-hour or so day—at a pace which would seem fast to anyone else, but was comfortable to one with his talent. He seldom raced, and then only at short distances.

Years later, Derek still does the same thing. He says his whole outlook on running has changed. No longer is it the grinding work that he barely tolerated. It is now "one of the bright spots" in his day. The pain is gone, the pleasure remains. Running is not his test but his therapy, not his trial but his reward, not his question but his answer.

You, too, can run like the man who once held a world record.

THE RUNNING ROUTINE

You may know Mark Nenow by his statistics. At the time this book was written, no one had ever run faster than Nenow for ten kilometers on the road. You should know the approach that led to his time of 27:22. Mimicking Mark won't give you the same results, but it may make you a more flexible runner—and I'm not talking about stretching exercises here.

Nenow and I seemed to have our roles confused when we appeared at a running clinic together. I'm supposed to be the fun-runner, yet I spoke of plotting every step to be taken and analyzing every move made. Mark is supposed to be the serious athlete, yet he talked of running without planning.

He spoke without notes but had plenty to say. He answered qwuestions with lots of "I don't knows," but his non-answers contained much wisdom.

Nenow can't tell you his weight and resting pulse rate because he never checks them. He doesn't want his blood tested or his muscles biopsied because the results might tell him something he doesn't care to know. He doesn't use a computer to determine his training schedule, relying instead on instinct to tell him what to do.

He didn't say as much, but probably can't be bothered to keep a diary. He enters competition with only the most general of plans: "to stick my nose in it and run with the leaders as long as I can. That way, I either make a breakthrough or die like a dog." He can't remember times from recent races, which indicates that past performances don't mean a great deal to him.

Mark Nenow is a refreshing throwback to a bygone era of low-tech training. He certainly works hard, running well over one hundred miles a week at a fast pace most weeks. You don't become a world record-holder without doing that kind of work. But the way he does it separates him from the majority of his contemporaries. Nenow concerns himself only with the generalities of training steadily and racing hard, and lets the specifics take care of themselves. He *lets* things happen instead of trying to *make* them happen.

Such looseness requires great confidence and a faith that the instincts guiding him are the proper ones. Nenow trusts himself to do the right things without help from a team of coaches and scientists, and without the backing of elaborate plans and logbooks.

His way doesn't always work. Instinct told him not to race between the world-record 10-K in April 1984 and the Olympic Trials that June; he thought he was getting too fit too soon. Instead of making the U.S. team as expected, Mark placed eleventh. Then he immediately ran this country's fastest 5000- and 10,000-meter races of the year.

Such quick recoveries from disappointment are as much a part of Nenow's approach as his surprising breakthroughs. Failures are less devastating when expectations aren't excessive, and successes are all the more satisfying when they aren't planned.

Nenow says all of his big improvements have come as "surprises." Because he doesn't set specific time goals, he sets no artificial limits on himself. He once passed the midpoint of a 10-K faster than his 5000-meter personal record. Others might think, "Uh-oh, I can't keep going at that pace," and then slow down. Nenow kept going and improved his 10-K time by nearly a minute.

Nenow may be short on knowledge of running theory and his own practice of it, but he is long on wisdom. Anyone with a little know-how can complicate something simple. Only a wise person can make the complicated simple.

Mark Nenow's lesson to us all is not to let the planning and analyzing get in the way of the doing and enjoying. Remember the story of the insect that thought too much.

> The centipede was happy quite
> until a toad in fun said,
> 'Pray which leg after which?'
> That worked her mind to such a pitch
> she lay distracted in a ditch,
> considering how to run."

CHAPTER NINETEEN

The Runs

I'm not big on goals. I'd rather take care of little matters and then let the big ones happen as a natural result, rather than dream of large happenings and worry about fitting little pieces into a grand plan.

As a runner, I have but one goal. No longer is it to break any personal records, or to race any specific times or distances. My goal is simply to become an old runner. What I want to do most is keep running far into the future.

Acts of God may prevent me from doing so. I have no control over those. What I can control are my own acts. This self-control takes the form of two promises to myself: (1) Keep nothing in my routine that interferes with the goal; and (2) Add nothing new that keeps me from getting where I want to go.

My routine has evolved over many years into one that promotes survival. I've lasted since 1958 with only the briefest of breaks. I've run for as many as four years without missing a day. As a number, 1400 straight days is unimportant. The significant fact is that I didn't *need* or want a day off in all that time.

The program that let me run that long without physical or mental lapses was basically sound, but it could have been better. It left me with frequent minor aches. It sometimes made me feel like I was running to satisfy the schedule instead of myself.

Two inspirations from very different directions led me to modify the daily routine. These came from Kenneth Cooper, the king of aerobics, and from Mark Nenow, the king of the world's 10-K road racers.

Dr. Cooper, as noted in earlier chapters, calls for limited amounts of running. Nenow, as reported in the introduction to Part Seven, runs on instinct. I needed changes in both directions.

Cooper has all the figures. He has studied hundreds of thousands of subjects in his Air Force and Aerobics Center laboratories. Thousands more readers of his books have told him their tales. His advice comes from personal as well as professional experience. He was his own first test subject. He raced the mile in high school and college, and later became a marathoner.

These experiments and experiences have led Cooper to the conclusion that the ideal training distance is two to three miles, the ideal frequency four days a week, and "anyone who runs more than fifteen miles a week is doing it for reasons other than fitness." For more than twenty years, Cooper has kept exact count on his own running totals. "I've averaged 4.6 days a week," he says, "logging 2.7 miles every time I go out." That also may help explain why he recommends three miles five days a week as his maximum for all fitness runners.

"I've completed my 20,000th mile of running," adds Cooper. "I think my fitness program has a lot to do with my health. I haven't missed a day of work due to sickness in thirty years." He doesn't say how many, if any, days of running he has missed due to injury. There couldn't have been many—if any—while he maintained such consistency.

Dr. Cooper offers compelling arguments. The grabber is that he has noticed a great increase in musculoskeletal injuries among runners who go more than a half-hour per run. At the same time, they gain little or nothing more than lower-total runners in cardiovascular benefits.

That may be true, but I am equally certain that many people—myself included—are willing to take slight risks because we run for very good reasons other than fitness. Maybe *in addition to fitness* would be a better term. We run for competition and recreation, and training and fun-running barely begin at the point where Cooper's prescription leaves off.

Fitness is still important to us, but perhaps our definition of it varies from Cooper's. We aren't so concerned with cardiovascular health as with avoiding the orthopedic problems that keep us from running.

With my goal—my only goal—of living to be an old runner, I have drawn upon Cooper's advice in revising my everyday approach slightly. I didn't go so far as to take two or three days a week off, or limit myself to two or three miles, or never go longer or fast. I cheat on the Cooper formula, but by less than before.

His upper limit of three miles translates to thirty minutes for most of the people in his audience. I cover more ground in that time, but who's counting? A half-hour is now my base. That's down by nearly one-third from my old quota.

This is not to say that I'll rigidly do a half-hour, give or take a few minutes, every day from here to eternity. I'm now enjoy more variety than I've known in years, thanks to my second source of inspiration. Mark Nenow's story introduces this part of the book. I'm not prepared to give up the written formulas (such as Tables 19.1 and 19.2) and records that Nenow successfully does without. But following his lead, I loosened up the routine that had become a rut.

Table 19.1 *Running Distance*

Daily runs ideally fall into the thirty- to sixty-minute time range. These comfortably paced efforts (see Table 19.2 for a personal definition of "comfortable") are long enough to be satisfying but not long enough to be exhausting. If you prefer to run by miles instead of minutes, the table lists the distances covered within the half-hour to hour time range at a particular pace. (Distances are rounded to the nearest tenth-mile.)

Your Pace per Mile	Distance Run in 30 Minutes	Distance Run in 60 Minutes
6:00	5.0 miles	10.0 miles
6:15	4.8 miles	9.6 miles
6:30	4.6 miles	9.2 miles
6:45	4.4 miles	8.9 miles
7:00	4.3 miles	8.6 miles
7:15	4.1 miles	8.3 miles
7:30	4.0 miles	8.0 miles
7:45	3.9 miles	7.7 miles
8:00	3.8 miles	7.5 miles
8:15	3.6 miles	7.3 miles
8:30	3.5 miles	7.1 miles
8:45	3.4 miles	6.9 miles
9:00	3.3 miles	6.7 miles
9:15	3.2 miles	6.5 miles
9:30	3.1 miles	6.3 miles
9:45	3.1 miles	6.2 miles

Table 19.2 *Running Pace*

The daily running pace should be "comfortable"—neither too fast nor too slow. The comfort zone for runs in the thirty- to sixty-minute range can be defined by current ten-kilometer racing ability. Calculate your most recent 10-K race pace, then add one to two minutes per mile. The result is your ideal running pace when not racing or training specifically for a race. The reverse is also true. In a 10-K race or speed training, you should go one to two minutes per mile faster than the running paces listed here.

Your 10-K Race Time	Your Pace per Mile	Your Fastest Training Pace	Your Slowest Training Pace
30:00	4:50	5:50	6:50
31:00	5:00	6:00	7:00
32:00	5:10	6:10	7:10
33:00	5:19	6:19	7:19
34:00	5:29	6:29	7:29
35:00	5:39	6:39	7:39
36:00	5:49	6:49	7:49
37:00	5:58	6:58	7:58
38:00	6:08	7:08	8:08
39:00	6:17	7:17	8:17
40:00	6:27	7:27	8:27
41:00	6:37	7:37	8:37
42:00	6:46	7:46	8:46
43:00	6:56	7:56	8:56
44:00	7:06	8:06	9:06
45:00	7:16	8:16	9:16
46:00	7:25	8:25	9:25

Table 19.2 Continued

Your 10-K Race Time	Your Pace per Mile	Your Fastest Training Pace	Your Slowest Training Pace
47:00	7:35	8:35	9:35
48:00	7:44	8:44	9:44
49:00	7:54	8:54	9:54
50:00	8:04	9:04	10:04
51:00	8:14	9:14	10:14
52:00	8:23	9:23	10:23
53:00	8:33	9:33	10:33
54:00	8:43	9:43	10:43
55:00	8:52	9:52	10:52
56:00	9:02	10:02	11:02
57:00	9:11	10:11	11:11
58:00	9:21	10:21	11:21
59:00	9:31	10:31	11:31

I was rutted in where, when, and what I ran. I had a set of seven courses, one for each day of the week, and always ran the same one on a Sunday, a Monday, and so on. I always ran between seven and eight o'clock in the morning. I always ran about forty-five minutes six days a week, always at a similar pace. I always tried to do something longer or faster on Saturdays.

No more. I still have standard courses, but their boundaries are less rigid than before, and I don't decide which way to go until my feet point me in a certain direction. The day of the "Wednesday course" is past.

I still do most of my running in the morning, but it can be anytime from dawn on (I still hate going out in the dark). Noon, afternoon, and even early evening runs now can occasionally add the spice of variety.

I still exceed a half-hour on many days, but I've quit planning to do more. If I cover the basic thirty minutes, I'm happy. If I go longer, I'm overjoyed. If I run less, I'm not disappointed because the reason for cutting back is obvious and stopping short is good preventive medicine.

I go longer or faster whenever I feel like it—not by a once-a-week schedule. That could now be two days in a row, or a whole month could pass without anything extra.

The extra efforts aren't training, which I define as specific preparation for races. Training still must be taken in small, infrequent doses (see Part Eight). What I'm doing in slightly longer and faster daily runs is a milder form of testing, a satisfying addition to the routine that doesn't add too much stress.

How much longer? Up to an hour, at the usual comfortable pace of one to two minutes per mile slower than current 10-K racing ability. I don't want the distance to be a struggle that will leave me too tired to run normally the next day.

How much faster? Not excessively so. I try to run at least one minute and not more than two minutes per mile faster than normal, and then only for a single mile in the midst of the usual half-hour run. I don't want the pace to be a strain that will leave me too stiff to run normally the next day.

Everyday running is not the time for getting tired and stiff. I save that experience for racing and race-like training, where these efforts count. Then I return to the daily runs for relaxation and recovery.

The
Plans

Galloway's Way

The star of this chapter and the several that follow is Jeff Galloway. He is a former Olympian, running-shop entrepreneur, author, lecturer, and a Southern gentleman in the old tradition of someone who'll help anyone who asks. I've gone to Galloway's running camps each summer to teach the campers, but have never failed to learn from Jeff.

One summer, Galloway completely changed my thinking about marathoning training when he drawled, "The only run that really counts is the long one. Make sure it is good and long, and you don't have to worry about what you do the rest of the time."

Galloway remarked that the biggest mistake that beginning marathoners make is training too often. They run too far in midweek, then are too tired to run far enough on the weekend. He advised taking no count of weekly mileage because it isn't important.

What counts for a runner trying to finish the first marathon, said Galloway, is the length of the long run. He recommended working up to full marathon distance in a long training session taken only once each week or two weeks, then recovering in between with no runs longer than eight miles. Someone trying to improve his or her time in subsequent marathons would make only one additional change: a speed-training session alternating with the distance efforts.

Galloway's system of mixing distance, speed, and recovery applies to all types of training. For instance, he believes triathletes get into trouble even more quickly than runners by running too much. The typical stress problems multiply, he says, when an athlete tries to mesh runs with swims and bike rides. He tells them to train good and long one day a week, good and fast another day, and to do little or no running the other days.

A running specialist preparing for any type race can adopt or adapt the Galloway formula. It blends the vital three vital ingredients—long enough, fast enough, and easy enough—into a productive schedule of running, training, and racing.

Running satisfies the "easy enough" requirement. It is what you do about ninety percent of the time, and is intended for recovery after a hard effort, rebuilding for the next one, and relaxing. As such, the runs should be only loosely planned, a la Mark Nenow (see Part Seven introduction and Chapter 19). Take care of generalities, such as wanting to cover at least a half-hour and no more than an hour, but let specifics take care of themselves.

Stan James, M.D., a prominent orthopedic surgeon and talented runner, has seen the damage runners inflict upon their bodies. He's even inflicted damage upon his own. He thinks one problem is a too-rigid daily running plan. Writing in *Runner* magazine, Dr. James notes, "Does everyone require a structured program? I don't think so. Rather, a general game plan with the specifics of each day's running determined just before the workout may be a better option. Often I don't know what my day's workout will be until I start. I let my body dictate distance and intensity. Simply playing off the body's feeling on a given day's workout may be the ultimate in running sophistication."

Training is where more careful planning comes in. You train to fulfill the "long enough" or "fast enough" requirements that are set by the race. Save the combination of full distance at full speed for the race, while training for speed and endurance separately. Train for your longest racing distance by going that far, but only at everyday running pace. Train for your shortest race's speed by going that fast, but for no more than half the race distance.

Racing is where long and fast come together, and the planning is done for you. The schedule tells you when, where, and how far you will run. Your competitive instincts give you no choice but to race the distance as fast as possible.

If you race regularly over a variety of short and long distances, you may never need to train. The racing itself will satisfy both the distance and speed requirements, and you'll need to spend the remaining time running easily.

Yiannis Kouros races more miles in one event than most of us will total in a career. The Greek regularly covers more than 600 miles in six straight days of racing, and he holds the world record for the relatively brief twenty-four-hour event. But if you imagine Kouros to be a training fanatic, think again.

In *Ultrarunning* magazine, Kouros reports that he rarely runs longer than twelve miles outside of races and never more than eighty miles a week. He considers training "an unavoidable evil. It must be done, but not in excess. The best training is racing."

It has been for me. All my best times came when I did no speedwork, no long training. I just raced long and short, often and well, and refilled the energy well with thirty- to sixty-minute runs between races.

Racing is more exciting than training. You have companions, crowds, split timers, aid stations. You have adrenaline flowing to draw more out of yourself than you could ever extract during a solo training effort.

If you are accustomed to racing frequently, if your area's race schedule gives you all the events you want, and if you aren't trying to peak for any one event, you can stay in shape for racing *by* racing. But those are big "ifs."

A runner unaccustomed to racing needs an intermediate step of training between easy running and all-out efforts. A runner with limited racing opportunities needs something to fill the gaps with training. A runner attempting to move to a new level of performance in one race needs specific preparation in training.

Serious runners combine all the elements—running, training, and racing; long enough, fast enough, and easy enough—into a single week. Rob de Castella, one of the world's leading marathoners, does just that almost year-round, every year. But runners without his abilities and ambitions may want to follow Jeff Galloway's lead and schedule only one big day a week, in the form of racing or training, and run easily on all other days (see table 20.1).

Table 20.1 *Running Week*

The recommended weekly routine outlined here mixes four ingredients: (1) *running* thirty to sixty minutes (less than a half-hour if injured or ill) at one to two minutes per mile slower than current ten-kilometer racing pace—possibly including up to a mile at one to two minutes faster than normal; (2) *training* at full race pace or full length, but not at top speed for the whole race distance; (3) *racing* at full effort all the way; (4) *optional* days, which may consist of normal training runs, shortened runs, or alternative activities such as hiking, biking, swimming, and cross-country skiing. A typical weekly pattern follows.

Day	Running Plan
Monday	train 30 to 60 minutes
Tuesday	train 30 to 60 minutes
Wednesday	train 30 to 60 minutes
Thursday	train 30 to 60 minutes
Friday	train 30 to 60 minutes
Saturday	race or train
Sunday	optional

Deek's Peaks

New Zealand's gift to training theory, delivered by coach Arthur Lydiard, was the concept of peaking once or twice a year for major competitions. Different periods of the annual or semi-annual cycle featured different emphases: distance, hills, speed sharpening, and finally racing. The system worked quite well for Lydaird-trained Olympic champions Peter Snell and Murray Halberg.

At least two runners from nearby Australia have taken an opposite approach. Ron Clarke, the most successful record-breaker of the last twenty years, gave little attention to peaks. He preferred instead to train consistently and to keep pushing his peak higher all the time. Clark was always ready to race.

One of the most successful marathoners of recent years, Australian Rob de Castella, follows a course similar to Clarke's. It is marked by continual upward progress rather than a series of peaks and valleys.

"Deek" has never been injured. He has averaged more than 100 trouble-free miles a week for the past five years. One reason for his good health is that he runs most of these miles on the soft paths of a forest. Another is that his heavily muscled legs appear to be almost injury-proof.

One preventive measure he doesn't take is stretching. Kenny Moore writes in *Sports Illustrated*, "De Castella habitually does the first mile of a run in about nine minutes." That's his way of working out the stiffness and soreness. "He isn't very flexible, yet seldom stretches."

If the Australian has a secret, it lies in the continuity and cumulative effects of his work. De Castella says, "You develop incredible strength through continuous running, and it's got a snowballing effect. Strength allows consistency, which brings more strength. Once you are injured, you are vulnerable to getting injured because of the inconsistencies in your training."

Dick Telford, an exercise physiologist who advises de Castella, adds, "People get injured when they alter the kind or intensity of their training. Since 1979, Rob has not changed his at all. He still runs his 400s [speed training] every Thursday. His Sunday [long-distance training] run is still the same pace. He has destroyed the myth that you have to intensify training to keep the body improving."

Like Ron Clarke before him, de Castella views peaking not as a steep climb toward a particular race, to be followed by a quick descent. He treats peaking as a steady climb that should go ever higher as the benefits of an unbroken string of days, weeks, months, and years grows.

Any runner looking to balance short-term racing results with long-term health and enjoyment of running should strive for similar consistency. One way is to adopt an all-purpose program (such as that described in table 20.2) that blends running, training, and racing in a recurring pattern.

Table 20.2 All-Purpose Program

This general schedule is designed for the frequent racer who races in the five-kilometer to half-marathon range. For more specific advice on training for these distances, and for those shorter and longer, see Part Eight.

In this program, you run through three-week cycles: one with a race from the short end of the range (lasting less than an hour) and emphasizing speed, a longer race (more than an hour) with the emphasis on endurance, and one without a race.

If no races are available, substitute a training session of similar speed or length. Train at the full pace of a speed race, but for no more than half the racing length. Train at the full time of the distance race, but at normal daily pace.

The other six days of the week are meant for relaxation and recovery. Thirty minutes is the suggested minimum run. You shouldn't exceed one hour on these days, since that turns running into *training*. An optional rest day is scheduled each week. Allow an extra one if you're unusually tired or sore.

Week	Days 1 to 5	Day 6	Day 7
1	30 to 60 minutes	speed race	optional
2	30 to 60 minutes	distance race	optional
3	30 to 60 minutes	no race	optional

The Records

Life Stories

Not many people get the chance to write their life story. Even fewer can look across their bedroom and see their life's work neatly packaged and stored in a bookcase. I do the former and have the latter. So can you.

I'm not speaking here of working as a writer who publishes books. I've been lucky enough to do that, and the results stand proudly on the the bedroom shelves. But those books have nothing to do with this chapter. The subject here is the running diary. I kept one long before my writing went public, and the diary has a life of its own—quite different from what I write for a living. You don't have to be a professional writer to profit from a diary.

My diary taught me almost all I know about running. Memories edit the past and often distort it, but numbers and words tell no lies. They tell me exactly what I did right and where I strayed—and why, if I look closely enough at the records.

Of course, I didn't suspect any of this would happen in November 1959 when I made my first entry in a little black book given to me by the Libertyville Lumber Company. I only intended to note what I ran each day.

The figures didn't mean much at first. Single days rarely do, either in running or reporting on it. The way the days add up is what counts, both on the road and on paper. Mine took months to add up enough for patterns to emerge. But when they did, they gave me a new game to play which was almost as exciting as the running itself.

I saw certain types and amounts of running giving certain results, good and bad. I learned more about training and racing from rereading my own scribbled history than from any of the books by the coaching giants of the 1950s and sixties. Franz Stampfl, Percy Cerutty, Fred Wilt, Ernst van Aaken, and Arthur Lydiard presented theories. The diaries listed my trial-and-error practice.

Many more days went toward trying and erring than toward real learning. But in between the insights, I fixed the habits of keeping records and, later, writing down observations each day. This took only a few minutes, but it added immeasurably to my knowledge of running and my excitement about it.

Lined up now on three shelves of my bedroom bookshelf are fat notebooks labeled "1984," "1983," and so on, all the way back to the original Libertyville Lumber Company diary marked "1959" on a brittle, yellowed piece of athletic tape. I'm prouder of them than of anything I've published because they are visible evidence of nearly every running step I've taken.

I urge everyone who runs to keep a diary. At the least, it gives you a place to brag and complain without boring anyone else. At best, they teach you more about running and about yourself. The most important book you'll ever read is the one you write yourself.

Days of Our Lives

Old habits never die; they just repeat themselves. It is out of habit, not will-power or dedication, that I have run for as long as four years without missing a day. I've forgotten how to stop. Writing is even more habit-forming. The last day I didn't put anything new into my diary was April 3, 1971.

Each day starts the same way. I write and then I run. The order was originally switched, until I realized the brain and left arm loosened up quicker than the legs did. The order doesn't matter. Running and writing are inseparable acts.

Today starts like all other days. I pull a fresh piece of college-lined notebook paper from the desk drawer and pick up a pen. Paper and pen are my tools; it's very important to me that they feel right. The paper must be college-ruled and the pen a cheap Bic with black ink, or the words don't look or flow like they should.

I label the top of the sheet with the date and day's writing topic and circle that notation. I write about whatever happens to be on my mind; today, it's the need for reading glasses. After hesitating a moment to find the starting line, I scribble the front and back full of words during the next half-hour or less.

I leave enough room at the bottom of the second page for a notation on the day's run. Today's report reads: "3/9—Fox: 37 min.-B (35°, 137 lbs.)." That is shorthand for a March 9th run on the Fox Hollow course, uphill to the turnaround point and down on the trip home.

Running time was thirty-seven minutes, which earned a "B" grade for quality. The temperature at the start was thirty-five degrees, and the pre-run weight stood at 137 pounds. All in all, a typical day. Anything atypical would have been noted in the parentheses.

The day's page goes into the binder marked "1985." One page doesn't seem to make it grow any, yet already this year the pages have collected to a thickness of nearly an inch. In writing as in running, consistency counts. Small daily efforts, taken regularly, add up to something big.

Diaries can function on three levels: as archives for facts, as places to analyze the facts, and as a place to exercise poetic license. As noted, my diary has evolved to the third level, but you'll probably want to concentrate on the first two.

Reporting

Diaries first serve the same purpose as home movies. So much of what runners do is invisible, gone behind us as soon as we pick up our feet, that we need a reminder of where we've been and what we did there. Diaries store old memories where we can see and touch them.

For instance, you can open your book to January 19, 1979, and recreate that day from the set of numbers and words on the page. You don't need many facts to trigger a chain-reaction of memories. The only two essentials are where and what you ran that day.

Any number of publishers are eager to have you put your figures into their prepared running diaries. But you don't really need anything that elaborate for reporting the basics. A calendar with a block of white space for each day will give you a month's worth of running on one page. So will a full-sized sheet of lined notebook paper.

I used a published diary for a few years of high school and college. Each page told a day's story in dozens of items. I filled the spaces religiously, listing everything that I put into myself and nearly everything that came out. If anyone wants to know what the South Page High School cafeteria served for lunch on November 22, 1960, I have the facts.

If nothing else, the years of putting checks and numbers into Wilt's pages taught me what was important to my running and what didn't matter very much. Eventually, I used so few of his boxes and wrote so many extra comments that I switched to blank paper. I finally reduced the essentials to a line or two.

I suggest you do the same. Keep the diary simple, and you're more likely to keep it current. Don't let it drown in trivia.

Analyzing

Days of running leave behind only individual footprints in a diary. You can't take much direction from them. But weeks, months, and years of running line up in a trail that points two ways. It shows where you have been before and where you might go next.

The trick in turning your history into a better future is learning to read that trail. Where on it did you move easily and quickly? What wrong turns did you take? Where were the potholes that tripped you? You smooth the path ahead by first looking back and processing the raw data that went into your book a day at a time.

Most runners do an elementary type of analysis: keeping weekly mileage or time totals. This begins to look at running as a set of connected steps. But a week isn't long enough, and the total amount of running doesn't tell enough. We react to our training and racing and recover from it slowly. To us, seven days is a very short time. If we measure our work by that period, the numbers may distort what we do.

For instance, you may normally do your long training on Sunday. But you're busy that day, and train a long distance on Saturday instead. This week's total—with its two big efforts—looks terrific. Next week's will appear puny without any long training, yet the training effects of both weeks are identical.

Another example: You raced a hard ten kilometers on Saturday. Ideally, you would give yourself all of the next week to recover. But you don't want to fall below your fifty-mile-a-week goal. So you overwork.

Monthly, rather than weekly, accounting takes care of these problems. Thirty-day periods are long enough to smooth out the energy spurts and slumps, race buildups and recoveries, and rearranged training days. A month's totals give a clearer picture of what you do. It clears up even more when you mix other key factors into the analysis (see Table 21.1 for a sample monthly summary).

1. *Daily average.* I prefer this to a total because the smaller numbers make more sense and the months are different lengths. Divide the distance or time total by the number of days, even if you don't run them all.
2. *Racing and training percentage.* How much of the month's running is significantly longer or faster than normal? I know now that I can't stand more than ten percent, and that I need at least five percent to race well. Determine your ideal figures by comparing them to PRs set and injuries suffered.
3. *Grade.* This is like a school grade-point average. Table 21.2 describes a grading system.
4. *Notes.* In months when I note races or routine-disturbing problems, I look to the numbers for reasons. They may not appear immediately, but they will eventually as monthly patterns repeat themselves.

Table 21.1 *Sample Monthly Summary—January*

Day	Run	Grade	Temperature	Weight
1	40 min.	B	69	139
2	30 min.	A	64	138
3	35 min.	B	53	138
4	45 min.	A	57	138
5	40 min.	B	62	138

Table 21.1—Continued

Day	Run	Grade	Temperature	Weight
6	35 min.	B	77	139
7	30 min.	B	55	139
8	33 min.	B	66	140
9	33 min.	B	57	138
10	36 min.	A	59	138
11	30 min.	B	51	138
12	35 min.	B	50	138
13	42 min.	B	65	137
14	43 min.**	A+	60	137
15	30 min.	B	50	139
16	30 min.	B	42	138
17	33 min.	B	53	137
18	40 min.	B	75	137
19	30 min.	B	60	137
20	31 min.	B	60	137
21	36 min.*	A	46	138
22	33 min.	B	48	139
23	36 min.	A	51	140
24	32 min.	B	57	139
25	32 min.	B	57	139
26	38 min.	B	50	139
27	36 min.	A	50	138

Table 21.1—*Continued*

Day	Run	Grade	Temperature	Weight
28	32 min.	B	48	138
29	34 min.	B	53	139
30	91 min.*	A	51	139
31	30 min.	B	51	139

Averages	37 min.	3.23	56	138
(Ranges)	(30–91)	(B–A+)	(46–77)	(137–140)

Notes:
1. ** 10-K race of 39:06
2. * training sessions: mile in 5:45 and long run of 1:31
3. 6.2 percent racing and training
4. Fastest pace for month: 6:18 per mile
5. No injuries or illnesses

Table 21.2 *Making the Grade*

Give each run, training session, or race a letter grade, as a teacher would score a test. Assign grades by the following subjective standards:

A+ = best efforts of the grading period in distance, speed, or both (usually occurring in races)

A = exceeded length or pace expectations

B = ran as expected

C = struggled to stay at normal levels

D = forced to cut back

F = didn't or couldn't run

At the end of each grading period (monthly is recommended), calculate a grade-point average by giving five points to each "A+," four to "A," three to "B," two to "C," one to "D," and zero to "F." Divide the total score by the number of days.

A reading above 3.00 means running is going right. Copy that program in the future. An average in the 2.00 to 2.99 range indicates that all is not well. Make subtle changes in the routine. A grade below 2.00 warns of serious trouble. Search out its cause and take immediate corrective action.

PART EIGHT

THE RUNNING TRAINING

When a runner races, one of two things happens. He or she does as expected or better, or does worse. In the first case, the usual reaction is, "If I did that well on X amount of training, think how much better I could do with more work." After a failure, the thinking goes, "The reason I did so poorly was that I didn't train enough. I'll have to start doing more."

Both runners are likely to make changes immediately. The changes almost always amount to overwork.

Many running theorists, Bill Bowerman chief among them, claim that more runners overwork than underwork. I'd estimate that nine out of ten serious runners sometimes run too much, and hurt their performances or themselves as a result.

I'm not just talking about hard work. All runners go too far or too fast once in a while. That's the nature of racing and training for races. The problem comes not from that work itself, but from working too hard *too often,* and not allowing enough to time recover and rebuild from the excesses.

I used to say that work and recovery are equal parts of the running puzzle. I've amended that to read that recovery is much more important—as much as *ten times* times more important. That's because we tear down quickly and repair slowly. As many as ten easy days are needed to overcome the effects of a single hard one.

I used to see how hard I could work, how much continual effort I could tolerate. After being hurt by that approach and seeing too many others suffer, I'm more interested now in how little hard work a runner can get by with and still get the results he or she wants. That formula may come down to as little as one big day each week, and maybe an occasional week when even that day is skipped.

Curiously, a man who inspired my thinking in terms of these minimums was an Olympian who was seeing how far he could push himself. I spent a week in Hawaii with Garry Bjorklund. He had flown there from winter-time Minnesota and was doing a two-hundred-mile training week.

I asked him what he would be doing if he were at home. He wasted no words: "Two hundred." He would have worn more clothes and would have enjoyed himself less, but he would have reached his quota even if he had stayed in Minneapolis. The Hawaiian trip was just a lucky break.

Bjorklund ran his two-hundred miles. It was the closest I've come to watching a man disintegrate before my eyes. The first day of the vacation, I met a normal, rational, energetic human being. By the next weekend, he could barely walk or talk straight.

Garry didn't do this every week. He couldn't have stood it. He explained that he ran by three-week cycles. This obviously was his big-mileage week. He would follow it with an easy week when he might do as little as five miles a day. The cycle had begun with a week emphasizing speed.

I am not a Bjorklund, nor do most of us have designs on Olympic teams, or the drive and ability to pursue such goals. But his basic pattern can be modified to fit the needs and tastes of almost anyone. It may come down to substituting the word *day* for *week*. Some runners thrive on as little as one big day a week.

- A *day* of speed the first week. This may be either a short race at full speed, or a training run at that pace for a reduced length.
- A *day* of distance the second week, taken either as a long race at full effort or a training run of about equal length but at a reduced pace.
- A third week free of anything unusually fast or long. This equals Bjorklund's recovery week.

Between the big days, *every* day is a recovery day. All runs stay in the comfort zones of both speed and distance.

CHAPTER TWENTY-TWO

The Tests

Longer, Faster, Easier

"The end to all our exploring," wrote T. S. Eliot, "is to arrive where we started and to know the place for the first time."

In other words, progress doesn't run in a straight line. It travels in a circle. I've run full circle. I'm back to doing what I did before I knew what to do. Now I know. I've tried everything else and can see that what I did instinctively in the beginning was right for me.

When I became a runner, instinct told me I couldn't race daily and should fill the spaces between races with easier runs. When I wasn't racing, I ran on the country roads. In Iowa, those roads are laid out in a checkerboard pattern. Each square is a mile to a side; four miles surround a section of farm land.

My typical run became a comfortably paced trip around a section. On good days, I might go to the next intersection before turning back, making the run six miles long. Rarely would I do more than that. The typical session lasted thirty to forty-five minutes.

The mix of these modestly long runs and weekly short races served me well. I raced my mile time down to 4:22. I never ran much faster, and have seldom felt healthier. Injuries appeared only when I got "smart" and deviated from the basic plan.

The age of innocence ended in 1961. I deviated greatly from that simple program in years to come. The long runs became much longer, and, for a while, a lot faster. The speedwork became much more frequent, complex, and difficult.

I was injured often, both from going too far and too fast. My racing times improved only marginally in the next few years, then all improvement ceased. By 1966, I had traveled to the farthest point from where I'd started. That's when I began the long trip back home.

That journey back to simplicity began with "LSD." The switch to long, slow distances came entirely on impulse. One summer day, I simply stopped training for speed and started running comfortably. In fact, LSD training was none of the above. I never ran very long or slow most of the time, and never kept track of distances, only times. I ran between thirty and forty-five minutes most days. At its best, this type of running wasn't "training."

In other words, I came back to doing just about what I'd done in high school, before I knew what to do. The only difference: I now raced at much longer distances—the marathon and occasionally beyond.

That racing had two effects on my running: (1) I sometimes needed longer training sessions to get ready for those races; and (2) the races took a lot more out of me, so I needed longer to recover between then.

I couldn't race or train long very often. But I tried anyway. Only later did I look back and see the damage these excesses did. They first robbed me of energy and enthusiasm, then performances suffered, and finally health itself was undermined. Without going into painful detail, I ran myself into foot surgery.

Only then did I see why. Only then did I discover that racing is a prescription item that only works when taken in small, measured doses. Only then did I see that LSD isn't a training system but a *recovery* system for filling the gaps between hard efforts.

I rechecked the old records, all the way back to the start—when I knew nothing but everything worked out okay. The figures of five and ten percent jumped out at me.

If I raced, or took long or fast training that mimicked racing, less than five percent of the time, I wasn't fit and sharp enough to race well. I felt clumsy and sluggish.

However—and this was my usual problem—when I went beyond ten percent, I slid downhill. Energy, enthusiasm, performance, and health deteriorated. The year all of the above hit and led to me the operating room, I raced fifteen percent of the time. Four months topped twenty percent, and during one binge I raced nearly one mile in every two!

The best racing came when I worked this hard at least five percent and no more than ten percent of the time. That's one minute or mile hard for every ten or twenty of recovery.

For example, the year 1968 stands out most sharply for its records. I set PRs from ten to thirty kilometers. Running nothing faster than seven and one-half-minute miles most of the time, I did a 4:27 mile on the track. Another time, I had a 4:28/15:18 double for one and three miles. I was cooking! On the other hand, the year is notable for what it *didn't* contain: no injuries, no illnesses.

The racing/training percentage during all of 1968 was 6.4. During the best months of mid-year, the figure was slightly lower. Was it a fluke, a one-time period of health and enthusiasm when I could have raced well no matter what I did? I don't think so. I have too many figures from other years to prove otherwise.

- Track season, 1960—my first time to win regularly: 6.2 percent.
- Cross-country season, same year—undefeated: 5.4 percent.
- Final high school track season—including a three-mile PR that was never broken: 6.3 percent.

I was doing things right in these early years without really knowing what I was doing. Once I thought I knew what to do, I usually did them wrong.

I'm sure I blew a 4:10 to 4:12 mile in college by getting too greedy. I began the month of April 1964 with a 4:18.2 race which, because of my error, would remain my fastest ever. I quickly followed that with a 1:55.7 half-mile in training—another PR—then 4:19.1 and 4:18.4 miles the next week. A few days later came a three-quarter-mile training effort in 3:08.7. That was far too much speed in too brief a period.

The day my teammates all made their breakthroughs in the mile, I couldn't compete because of a calf injury. That month totaled 10.2 percent racing and race rehearsals.

In all cases listed here, good and bad, my typical daily runs averaged well under an hour at a comfortable pace. All the difference was in the dosage of racing and race-specific training.

After the surgery of 1973, the plan changed radically. It became almost 100 percent easy. I shied away from racing—at first because it was too painful, then because I feared a rerun of the old injury (a similar problem with the other foot) and finally because racing lost some of its attraction as fields grew into the thousands.

Something was missing from my running, and I've now replaced it. While I don't enter many races, I again pretend to race regularly through speed and distance training. Now it is an end in itself rather than preparation for competition.

My experiments with too much and too little racing and training led to the formulas that make up Chapters 22, 23, and 24. Essentially, they call for training once a week (in the absence of a weekly race). Distance rehearsals involve running the length of the race at a slower pace. Speed rehearsals are taken a race pace but for a shorter distance.

Personally, I'm content with races lasting an hour or less. At sixty minutes, running becomes *training* for me. An occasional hour of training is long enough.

Five kilometers is the shortest I care to race. The pace at that distance rarely dips much below six minutes per mile any more. So my speed training of a mile at a little under 6:00 is fast enough.

On the vast majority of days when I'm not training or racing, I keep the runs easy enough to allow recovery from the hard work. These runs now are closer to a half-hour than an hour.

The section lines of Iowa are long gone, but I'm back to running pseudo-sections of about four miles most days. Mile racing is years behind me, but I'm again semi-racing miles. I'm back to where I started. And I know the place—really know it—for the first time.

Balancing the Extremes

The evolutionary course I outlined for myself isn't just my story but the history of the sport in my running lifetime. What might be called "progress" is nothing more than regular pendulum swings back and forth from one extreme to another.

Runners, myself included, are extremists. We take a good technique and spoil it by carrying it too far. Nowhere are the pendulum swings wider and more regular than in training theory and practice. I've gone and have seen thousands of other runners reach the extreme of speed and then distance.

As the pendulum swung in the late 1950s and early sixties from sensible to excessive speed, the sore-legged victims (myself among them) looked for relief. New Zealanders offered one source. Runners from that country with fewer people than Chicago won two races and placed third in another at the Rome Olympics, then later rewrote the world records. We heard that Arthur Lydiard trained all of them, regardless of their racing distance, like marathoners.

What Lydiard did, in fact, was prescribe distance training—100 miles a week at a pace neither too fast nor too slow—for a few months each year. He followed that endurance work with intensive hill and track work.

However, runners who had overdosed on speed saw only the distance message. The pendulum swung back in that direction. We moved off the track and onto the roads. We carried Lydiard's good ideas to extremes.

A few months of road work became a full year of it; the speed portion of the recipe was forgotten. A moderate pace became a slow one; anything to get in those miles. One-hundred-mile weeks became 120 and 150 and more; more had to equal better.

It didn't, of course. We overdosed on distance as we had on speed. We got hurt and discouraged as surely by long mileage as we had by hard pace. The lesson from the last twenty-five years has been that too much of anything—speed or distance—equals nothing.

As the pendulum now swings back toward speed work, I hope it will stop somewhere between the extremes of distance and speed. I hope we can strike a sensible balance between those two necessities, remembering that most of the weight in that balance always goes to running that is neither very long nor very fast. (Table 22.1 suggests one such combination.)

Table 22.1 *Training Month*

This suggested plan points toward one race a month, typically in the eight-kilometer to half-marathon range. Races shorter than 5-K may require an additional speed day each week, while events longer than the "half" may demand additional weeks for building up distance before the race and extra recovery time afterward.

Two weekly training sessions, one long and one fast, precede the race. Distance work should approximate the race length but not its pace. Speed work, at up to half the race distance, should match the race speed; this training may be taken at a steady pace or interval-style. A weekend of recovery follows the race.

Week	Big Day	Other Days
1	long test, full race time*	30 to 60 minutes
2	fast test, half race length	30 to 60 minutes
3	race	30 to 60 minutes
4	no race or test	30 to 60 minutes

---

*If the race is to be shorter than the average training run, replace the distance test with another fast one.

CHAPTER TWENTY-THREE

The Distance

Adding Distance

(Advice in this chapter centers on the marathon, and largely on new marathoners. However, the principles are applicable to anyone wishing to extend his or her training and racing distances.)

Despite a certain devaluation of mileage that has occurred during the running boom, the marathon remains the Mount Everest of the sport: a peak that every runner dreams of scaling at least once.

If you haven't already gone to the top, that mountain may be easier to climb than you think. If you can race a 10-K, you can with a few more months' training tack on the additional twenty miles.

Sound farfetched? Well, consider this: Honolulu conducts one of the country's largest marathons each December. More than 10,000 runners enter, and all but a few dozen complete the course.

Other marathons are larger, but the remarkable feature of Honolulu is the large number of first-timers. Most of them are graduates of the Marathon Clinic founded by two physicians, Jack Scaff and John Wagner.

Starting in March, hundreds of would-be marathoners gather each Sunday for running lessons and a training run. These aren't hardened veterans of the sport; the majority are new runners or novices who have never before run farther than ten kilometers. The Clinic boasts that ninety-eight percent of the people who stick with the program finish the Honolulu Marathon. (That program is similar to the one outlined in Table 23.2.)

Marathon Schedule

Credit the ideas that follow to Jeff Galloway (who was introduced in Chapter 20). To appreciate the value of the Galloway marathon plan, you first must know the qualities of its author, the marathoner and the man. He has viewed running from every angle, and he now passes along the lessons from more than twenty years on the roads.

Jeff ran his first marathon at age eighteen. He recalls that "weekly mileage of thirty barely prepared me. But I was falsely consoled by the thought that others in the race were worse prepared than I. The first ten miles felt great. By fifteen miles, the distance of my longest previous run, I was tired. At twenty-one miles, I was so tired I couldn't logically recognize that I should quit. Instinct kept me going, so I walked most of the last five miles."

Logic might have driven Galloway into early retirement, but instead it sent him looking for better methods. He made the Olympic team in 1972, and nine years later, at age thirty-five, improved his PR to 2:15.

More importantly, Galloway had by then refined his training ideas to the point where he was ready to talk and write them out. He is a rare runner of elite class who knows how to advise the little people of the sport.

Jeff speaks frequently to prospective marathoners. One exchange that occurred during a speech years ago is lodged in his memory.

"I was giving a clinic on training. When someone asked about training for a marathon, I responded with the usual advice: Increase weekly mileage to sixty-five or seventy, with a twenty-miler each week for about four weeks.

"A non-'marathon-looking' person in the audience asked if one could run three miles a day and train for the marathon just by extending the long run to twenty-four miles or so. I said this didn't seem like enough training and that he might hurt himself on that sort of program.

"This fellow replied that he was currently using this program for his *fifth* marathon and hadn't been injured yet. I swallowed my 140-mile-a-week pride and asked him some questions."

Those answers and Galloway's later work with hundreds of new marathoners led him to radically revise his thinking about total mileage and long runs. He now says weekly mile-counting is unimportant, if not outright dangerous, because it urges people to increase their mileage on days when they should be relaxing. However, he says he can't overemphasize the value of long training runs taken every other week.

"I'm convinced," he says, "that the greatest causes of injury are increasing total mileage too quickly and maintaining long mileage for too many weeks without rest."

Galloway's marathon plan, a masterpiece of simplicity and practicality, avoids both problems by mixing a few very long runs in among lots of short ones. Its two cornerstones:

1. A long run on alternate weekends, increasing by gentle steps from just above one's current peak on up to the total time that the marathon is expected to take.
2. Lots of "filler" between the big efforts, resting one or more days a week and running only three to five miles on the other days "to make sure you recover between long runs."

Jeff says, "I recommend this program which avoids much of the risk of typical marathon training, while still giving excellent results. Scores of three-mile-a-day runners have shown me they can finish the marathon without hitting any wall—much less the fortress I ran into. They added the one key ingredient I lacked: a long run gradually increasing to marathon distance. They also taught me the importance of easing up between long runs, and coming to them eager and rested."

Runs as brief as thirty minutes satisfy that second requirement. You can start meeting the first one simply by pointing your long runs up that slope toward Everest.

Marathon Training

Increasing distances safely would normally take a long time—as much as six months, according to the Galloway formula of advancing by a mile or less per week. However, you can cheat that formula and still stay in one piece.

Tom Osler, another of the sport's resident geniuses, tells how. Osler was so heavy and slow as a young runner that his friends mocked him with the nickname "Turtle." He was forced to make up with cunning what he lacked in ability. Tom was successful enough in this quest that he won several national long-distance championships, and he isn't one to keep his hard-earned lessons secret.

Osler states flatly that anyone can go right out today, without any special preparation, and double his or her longest non-stop distance. If you have run steadily for ten kilometers, you can instantly make it twenty. If your current high is an hour, you can last for two. If a half-marathon is your best, you can complete a marathon.

The trick, says Osler, is to take walking breaks. "Wait a minute," you say. "I've had to walk in my runs, and I can hardly start again." That's because exhaustion forced you to stop; energy and enthusiasm were gone.

Osler's breaks are different. You take them voluntarily, *before* you tire, as a means of stretching available resources. You run fifteen, twenty, or twenty-five minutes, then walk five—perhaps drinking or stretching during the breathers. You accomplish larger amounts of work by breaking it into small pieces than by tackling it all at once. (Your current distance limits determine the need to walk. See Table 23.1 for guidelines.)

Table 23.1 *Distance Training*

Ken Young, former American record holder at a number of long distances and now director of the National Running Data Center, calculated the "collapse-point theory." It assumes that a runner will hit "the wall" at about triple the length of his or her average daily run. For instance, someone averaging forty-five minutes a day might run into trouble at about two hours.

The "collapse" theory offers a valuable training guideline. Compute that average from at least the past month, dividing the total amount of running by the total number of days (even if you didn't run everyday). Stop well short of your "wall," limiting the non-stop runs to twice the time of the average training run.

The stopping point can be extended significantly by inserting a five-minute walking break at least every half hour. Author and ultramarathoner Tom Osler maintains that a runner can go up to twice as far with the walks as without them. Adjust your figures upward by that amount when taking breaks.

Run at or near normal training pace (one to two minutes per mile slower than current 10-K racing ability), and count the walking breaks toward total time periods.

Daily Average	Safe Limit Non-Stop	"Collapse" Non-Stop	Safe Limit with Walks	"Collapse" with Walks
30 min.	1:00	1:30	2:00	3:00
35 min.	1:10	1:45	2:20	3:30
40 min.	1:20	2:00	2:40	4:00
45 min.	1:30	2:15	3:00	4:30
50 min.	1:40	2:30	3:20	5:00
55 min.	1:50	2:45	3:40	5:30
60 min.	2:00	3:00	4:00	6:00

The program in Table 23.2 combines the wisdom of Osler and Galloway. You jump immediately from a one-hour peak to two hours, then move up by quarter-hour increments every other week to reach three hours. The final push comes in the marathon itself, where walking is not prohibited but the goal is to eliminate it.

Once that goal is accomplished, the next one probably will be finishing the next marathon *faster*. Table 23.3 gives suggestions for making improvement possible.

Table 23.2 *First-Marathon Training*

Your goal as a first-timer should be to finish the race without encountering any "wall." To accomplish that, put aside for now all thoughts of speed—both in the race and in the training for it. Concentrate on mimicking the experiences of the marathon in the once-weekly long training session.

This schedule is designed for runners who haven't regularly gone beyond two hours in racing and training. (If you have a more extensive background, Table 23.3 may better suit your needs.) On alternate weeks, (1) train two hours and more, with a five-minute walking break every half-hour; and (2) train about half that amount, without walks. Base the maximum length of this training on your predicted race time.

While the program applies specifically to the marathon, it can be adapted to a range of long-distance races: those lasting more than two hours, or twenty-five to thirty kilometers and up for most runners.

Week	Big Day	Other Days
1	two hours with walk breaks	30 to 60 minutes
2	one hour without walks	30 to 60 minutes
3	2:00 to 2:15 with walks	30 to 60 minutes
4	1:00 to 1:15 without walks	30 to 60 minutes
5	2:15 to 2:30 with walks	30 to 60 minutes
6	1:15 to 1:30 without walks	30 to 60 minutes
7	2:30 to 3:00 with walks	30 to 60 minutes
8	1:15 to 1:45 without walks	30 to 60 minutes
9	2:45 to 3:30 with walks	30 to 60 minutes
10	1:30 to 2:00 without walks	30 to 60 minutes
11	3:00 to 4:00 with walks	30 to 60 minutes
12	one hour maximum	30 to 60 minutes
13	marathon race	about 30 minutes

Table 23.3 *Faster-Marathon Training*

Your goal after finishing a marathon will be to run that distance faster. Accomplishing it requires mixing long training and fast training.

This schedule, written for runners who have trained less than two hours in recent months, is designed to increase your maximum distance over two months, while keeping in mind the importance of occasional faster runs.

The special ingredients: (1) distance training of two hours and more (maximum amount based upon your predicted race time), with five-minute walking breaks available as an option; and (2) speed training at projected race pace but not more than half the racing distance.

While this program applies specifically to the marathon, it can be adapted to a range of long-distance races: those lasting more than two hours, or twenty-five to thirty kilometers for most runners.

Week	Big Day	Other Days
1	2:00 to 2:30	30 to 60 minutes
2	fast 10-K	30 to 60 minutes
3	2:30 to 3:00	30 to 60 minutes
4	fast 15-K	30 to 60 minutes
5	2:45 to 3:30	30 to 60 minutes
6	fast half-marathon	30 to 60 minutes
7	3:00 to 4:00	30 to 60 minutes
8	fast 10-K	30 to 60 minutes
9	marathon race	about 30 minutes

CHAPTER TWENTY-FOUR

The Speed

Picking Up Speed

(This chapter focusses on people who are graduating from running to racing at the most popular distance, ten kilometers. However, the advice applies to improving speed in other events and to more advanced runners.)

The difference between running and racing is measured by effort and pace. You work harder in a race than in everyday runs because everyone around you is doing the same; the crowd pulls you along. If your work is paying off as it should, you run a minute or more per mile faster than you normally would.

Just as your ability to cover distances improves rapidly during the early stages of a running program, so will your racing talent make dramatic leaps forward as you learn to train and race faster. Speed improves even more rapidly than endurance does, and on much smaller and less-frequent dosages.

As a new racer, you can break personal record after record while applying the speed just one day each week. This may take the form of an actual race, where you get a direct payoff on your investment. But you probably need to supplement your racing schedule with the race-like training defined in this chapter. Either way, one fast day each week is adequate for all but the most serious athletes.

The best way to measure improvement is to race the same distance repeatedly. That distance most likely will be ten kilometers, since it is contested most frequently. The reason for its popularity may be that 10-K is the perfect length for a race: long enough to provide a good workout, but short enough for runners to survive without hitting a "wall"; long enough to race without doing the excessive speed training of a miler, but short enough to finish without training the great distances of a marathoner; long enough to let you know you've earned your performance, but short enough to let you race again within a week or two.

You already run comfortably in the thirty- to sixty-minute range, and that's exactly how long it takes to finish a 10-K. You're well prepared to go that far, and you've had some introductory lessons in running fast at a shorter distance. The two factors of endurance and speed combine perfectly in a ten-kilometer race.

Speed Schedule

Elizabeth Stronge happens to be an experienced long-distance runner capable of winning races. She is also one top athlete worth emulating, because she speaks with the voice of a fun-runner.

The young woman from Alabama divides her running into two distinct parts: running and racing. The line between the two never blurs. She runs simply, at modest distances and paces, and will tolerate no training methods which might make her running a second job.

Stronge only shifts gears when she races. Then she runs as hard and fast as she can, including a sub-36:00 10-K and sub-3:00 marathon. She says her relaxed training leaves her looking forward to the racing efforts instead of dreading them as "more of the same hard work."

"I never know how far I run," she says of her daily runs. "I go by how I feel. I just look at the clock when I leave the house and again when I return."

More serious runners often tell Elizabeth how much better she would be if she worked harder on her speed between races. "I just smile and continue running the way I prefer. I think running is a wonderful thing if it doesn't become a chore."

That is the kind of balanced outlook you should seek. Race, by all means. Race regularly and race hard, and take pride in every second of improvement that you earn with your own sweat. But don't allow racing to become the tail that wags the dog. Race-like efforts can be productive and fun when kept in their place, which is one day each weekend. They can grow dreary and destructive when they spill over that limit.

Use the two distinct gears: running and racing. The first is easy, the second hard. The first builds up, the second tears down. The trick to successful, enjoyable, lasting running is to repair faster than you tear. Race no more than once a week, and do no race-like training on days meant for recovery and rebuilding.

Speed Training

Speakers on the running-advice circuit will tell you that they hear three questions more than all others.

- "How do I start running?" That was once your question, and you've lived the answers.
- "How do I train to finish a marathon?" Chapter 23 addresses that question, after first noting the attraction of this Mount Everest of the sport which must be climbed "because it is there."
- "How do I improve my speed?" You know how racing feels, and now you want to race faster.

Marlene Cimons is a nationally known writer whose byline appears regularly in running magazines and in one of the country's leading newspapers. However, her running skills don't yet match her writing talents.

Cimons came to the sport rather recently. After going through the learning phase, she entered racing via the familiar ten-kilometer route and soon finished her first marathon. Then she realized "I could run forever, but my times in the 10-K had stalled." She pleaded with me, "How do I get off this plateau?"

I told Marlene she was a one-pace runner. "You run eight-minute mile pace in your daily training. You run eight minutes in short races. You run eight minutes in long races. If I dropped you out of an airplane, you'd probably fall to the ground at eight minutes a mile."

Marlene needed a crash course in speed. I recommended that she go to a track once a week and run a mile at least a minute faster than her stalled pace. "To keep from tearing yourself apart, divide the mile up into four separate laps and walk a lap in between. Take a total time for the fast segments, and let me know the results."

Cimons gave weekly reports. She broke seven minutes the first week, but the test left her tired and sore. Then she began to adapt. The times improved, and the discomfort waned.

After a few weeks of this, Marlene entered another ten-kilometer race. She bettered her personal record by almost three minutes. Nothing else had changed in her running life except the addition of that single fast mile once a week.

No one can promise you improvement this dramatic: thirty seconds per mile in less than two months. Breakthroughs of about ten seconds a mile are more common, but this still adds up to a full minute for ten kilometers. Not many runners get the chance to improve so much, so quickly.

(For suggestions on how fast to train and how to train fast, see Table 24.1. Advice on preparing for a 10-K is contained in Table 24.2, while Table 24.3 covers the increasingly popular half-marathon.)

Table 24.1 *Speed Training*

How you train fast depends on how fast you run you each day. The pace of daily running sets your speed limits. Before training for speed, estimate the pace per mile at which you normally run and the pace the pace of your upcoming race (you should train at least that fast). Then determine how to train, steadily or interval-style. Walking breaks are unnecessary at paces up to one minute per mile faster than the daily rate, are optional between one and two minutes faster, and are strongly recommended at two-plus minutes.

Running Pace	Pace without Walk Breaks	Walk Breaks Optional	Walk Breaks Required
6:00	5:00–5:59	4:00–4:59	sub-4:00
6:15	5:15–6:14	4:15–5:15	sub-4:15
6:30	5:30–6:29	4:30–5:29	sub-4:30
6:45	5:45–6:44	4:45–5:44	sub-4:45
7:00	6:00–6:59	5:00–5:59	sub-5:00
7:15	6:15–7:14	5:15–6:14	sub-5:15
7:30	6:30–7:29	5:30–6:29	sub-5:30
7:45	6:45–7:44	5:45–6:44	sub-5:45
8:00	7:00–7:59	6:00–6:59	sub-6:00
8:15	7:15–8:14	6:15–7:14	sub-6:15
8:30	7:30–8:29	6:30–7:29	sub-6:30
8:45	7:45–8:44	6:45–7:44	sub-6:45
9:00	8:00–8:59	7:00–7:59	sub-7:00
9:15	8:15–9:14	7:15–8:14	sub-7:15
9:30	8:30–9:29	7:30–8:29	sub-7:30
9:45	8:45–9:44	7:45–8:44	sub-7:45

Table 24.2 Ten-Kilometer Training

Most runners have no problem with the 10-K distance; it's lack of speed that holds them back. With this fact in mind, this schedule is designed to improve your speed during a month of special training and racing at short distances.

The program assumes that you have not been racing regularly at distances 10-K and less, and that you have taken no recent speed training. (If you're more experienced at speedwork, you may wish to add another speed-training session each week, race all-out at shorter distances, or both.)

The training is a race rehearsal, run at or slightly faster than your goal pace for the 10-K, but not more than half the racing distance. These sessions may be taken either as non-stop runs or interval-style (with walking/jogging between fast segments, but not counting the recovery breaks toward the total distance).

While this is labeled as a 10-K program, it can be adapted to the range of short-distance races lasting less than an hour, or 5-K to 15-K for most runners.

Week	Big Day	Other Days
1	train mile/1500 meters at 10-K pace	30 to 60 minutes
2	train 2 miles/3000 meters at 10-K pace	30 to 60 minutes
3	train 3 miles/5000 meters at 10-K pace	30 to 60 minutes
4	race 10 kilometers	30 to 60 minutes

Table 24.3 *Half-Marathon Training*

The increasingly popular "half" requires special emphasis on both endurance and speed. Few runners go this far regularly, and few commonly travel at half-marathon race pace.

The schedule assumes that you have not been racing regularly at this and shorter distances, and have taken no recent training at race length or longer. Special ingredients: (1) long training at the projected time of your race but at normal training pace, and (2) fast training at race pace but not more than half the racing distance.

While this program applies specifically to the half-marathon, it can be adapted to a range of middle-distance races: those lasting between one and two hours, or fifteen to thirty kilometers for most runners.

Week	Big Day	Other Days
1	train at full H-M race time	30 to 60 minutes
2	train 10-K at H-M race pace	30 to 60 minutes
3	train at full H-M race time	30 to 60 minutes
4	train 10-K at H-M race pace	30 to 60 minutes
5	race half-marathon	about 30 minutes

THE RUNNING COMPETITION

I won't name the race or its host city. But I can tell how the awards ceremony there turned into a confrontation.

The start had been messy and late. The results had been slow coming together, and now the awarding of prizes was running a half-hour behind scheudle. Many of the winners saw their awards handed to someone else. Angry shouts filled the air. As the reader of wrong information, I became an easy target for the anger.

These mixups were later corrected. The published results listed the true winners, who now are wearing the watches given them as prizes. All is forgiven, but not forgotten. For my part, I'm wary of ever being caught in such an ugly scene again. In fact, I'm left wondering if awards and awards ceremonies aren't more trouble than they are worth.

Programs of this sort can be a great excuse to hang around and socialize after racing. They provide a rare chance to see the top runners up close and standing still. This is the traditional way of recognizing and rewarding excellence.

The trouble begins when the prize becomes more valuable than the process of winning it, and the ceremony comes to mean more than the race itself. I don't say this as an envious outsider who never had his moment on the victory stand. I did more than my share of winning as a boy. None of the victories was major, but I won dozens of races at a time when finishing first was still the only way to be recognized as a winner. I collected enough ribbons, medals, plaques, and trophies to fill a closet.

Early success no doubt helped fire my excitement for the sport. But prizes weren't what got me started or kept me going. I ran into my third year before winning anything of substance. By then, finishing in a fast time was already more important than finishing first—and far more valuable than any prize I might receive for it. The awards never meant as much to me as the results I wrote in my logbook after racing. As noted in Chapter 21, the records are all lovingly preserved and displayed.

By contrast, the awards are scattered. Some rest in a box in my closet. My mother and brother in Iowa have custody of others. Most are lost forever, the victims of neglect. I never look at the race prizes that remain with me. No race prize is on display at my home/office.

Perhaps the running awards mean so little to me because, in the simpler days of the 1960s, the awarding of them was done so unceremoniously. As I recall, the usual procedure in high school track was to hunt up a minor official at table on the infield and ask for the prize. If you didn't ask, you didn't get anything. There were no announcements, no bugles, no drums, no applause. Awards were an afterthought.

I learned early that the race is its own reward. If it goes well, no further evidence of victory is needed. If the time is unsatisfying, no trinket can make it seem better.

All these years later, I can't remember a single awards ceremony. There may have been some that tried to mimic the Olympics, but even those were cheap imitations of the real celebration that occurred when I first heard my time.

I can't remember how I received awards or what prizes went with which races. But all these years after the first race, I can still tell you every significant time I ever ran. Those were the rewards that mattered. Those are the ones everyone can win.

I read with amusement about the endless subdividing of categories going on now in an attempt to give more people the chance to win a prize. Age groupings, categories for the handicapped, for the sexes, even for weight classes grow so numerous that we're approaching what, ironically, we've always had: a way we all can win. Time can make a winner of everyone.

The Preview

Final Days

Herbie Hamilton and Byron Moore were ready for their first marathon. They had trained enough and knew what to expect in the race. But the running partners from Louisiana didn't know what to do in the lull between the end of hard training and the start of hard racing.

"What should we do the week before the marathon?" they asked me. "What should we eat? How much should we run, if any? How should we prepare on the day of the race? What do we wear if it is cold? Do we tape our feet or use Vaseline on our legs? This is our first one, and we are very excited. We would appreciate your experienced suggestions."

The first thing I told them was that experienced runners get excited, too. We feel impatient, awkward, and confused in the last days and hours before races. Every suggestion I give, I've learned from mistakes I made repeatedly when excitement overcame good sense.

The two most sensible and most ignored rules about the final days are *don't train* and *don't experiment*. I don't say you must stop running entirely; just don't do anything more to rehearse for this race. It's too late. You don't get stronger tomorrow by working hard today. You use what you did last week, last month, even last year. Training benefits add up slowly. You can't cram the last few days with all the work you can stand, expecting to make up for what you skipped earlier. But it is never too late to tire yourself so much that you can't exploit your good training.

Other than stopping training and keeping the running easy in the week before a race, stay with familiar routines. This is not the time to experiment with new diets or drinks, new shoes or clothes. When in doubt about changing anything, *don't*.

Don't eat to run better. Eating is like training. You aren't going to help yourself much in the last week, but it isn't too late to hurt. Forget the dietary tricks. Forget about eating and drinking anything you haven't already tested before training sessions and found to be okay.

For similar reasons, don't experiment with shoes and clothing. I don't switch to racing shoes and advise you not to either. The time when you put the most stress on your feet and legs is not the time to make them adapt to a new footfall. Two tips: Race in your everyday running/training shoes that you know won't hurt you, and *never* break in new shoes of any kind in a race.

The guiding principle here is the same for everything you wear. Put on nothing in races until it has passed the tests of both your longest and fastest training sessions.

Final Hours

You wake up, stand on the forward edge of the day, and tell yourself it is a day like any other: twenty-four hours long, with the same sunrise and sunset as always. You tell yourself, "A billion Chinese don't care what I do today." You say these things to calm yourself.

It isn't working. You know and you care that today is The Day, *Race Day;* day of mystery, of anticipation, of dread. You made yourself a promise about this day weeks or months ago. You counted down the days as you prepared for it. You'll bore your family and friends with stories of what you did today.

But what will you do today? You can't know until you race, of course, so you wait . . . and wonder . . . and worry.

You feel the urge to do something, anything, but you aren't sure what. Uneasiness leads to aimless motion, confusion to mistakes. Because you neither want to waste motion today nor make mistakes, you need a plan. Make it up before the big day arrives, and keep it simple enough so you follow it automatically in the final hours—a time when you aren't sure you can remember how to tie your shoes.

1. *Get up early.* You may have to jump right from bed into a run on other days, but you shouldn't race that way. You risk injury by racing while stiff or sore; you surely give away too much time. Most distance races are scheduled in the morning—some very early—so get up several hours earlier, even if it means beating the dawn. Take a walk in the fresh air to wake up and loosen yourself. Perhaps take a shower for the same reasons. You won't miss the lost hours in bed if it means saving some minutes in the race.
2. *Stay close to the bathroom.* Your plumbing is twice as busy as usual. This extra activity is a natural part of race day, so don't worry about the amount. Just make sure you have a place to dispose of it. You don't want to carry to the starting line anything that might want out as you race.

3. *Eating is optional.* Do whatever you normally do. If you typically run in the morning, eight to twelve hours or more after your last meal, race that way. Don't eat. You know you won't collapse from malnutrition at the halfway point. If you're used to eating before running, take what you know you can tolerate. You should realize, though, that all you're doing is filling an empty place; you aren't getting much new energy this late.

4. *Drinking is essential.* Even on cool days, racers throw off liquids at an alarming rate. This starts before the race, for reasons given in Point 2. You might already be down a quart or so of liquid as you start. Fluid loss while running is inevitable, but you don't have to give it a headstart. Drink your way to the starting like, making sure you replace much of what your nerves are flushing out. Take small amounts, often.

5. *Remember shoes and shorts.* The essential items are the easiest ones to forget when packing for a race. Put on the shorts and shoes at home, and wear them out of the house. That way, you know you have them. You can borrow any old shirt if you forget yours, and you don't need much else.

6. *Arrive early, if you drive.* Know your route, find someone to take you, and allow plenty of time. If you must travel more than an hour on the day of the race, plan extra time after arrival to shake out the kinks of the trip. Give yourself an hour beyond the time you need for signing up and warming up.

7. *Sign up first.* Part of being a racer is enduring frustrating waits as officials take care of paperwork. Do your waiting in line as soon as you can and as little as you must. Check in before you start to warm up; don't interrupt your pre-race concentration for this. Pick a time when crowds are small, get in the shortest line, do your business, then hurry away to a calmer place.

8. *Sample the course.* Walk or just stand and look at small parts of it; don't run on it. Race day is too late for a complete tour. Your confidence is shaky enough without exposing it to every mile and hill. Distances seem twice as long and climbs twice as steep now as they will when you race them, so save those experiences for later. Just know where the starting line is, and if the finish is somewhere else. Find out exactly how you come in at the end, when exhaustion may confuse you. Ask where the time checkpoints and aid stations will be.

9. *Avoid the crowds.* Part of warming up for a race is simply thinking about it. You think best alone. If you have time before arriving and checking in, isolate yourself as much as possible and rest. When the active part of warming up begins, do it by yourself, too. Even if you don't want to be a loner, others may. Respect their privacy.

10. *Start hot or stay cool?* The choice depends on the distance you race. The shorter and faster the event, the more you must run before it starts. The longer it is, the less preliminary running you need. Before a mile race, for instance, take what amounts to a normal day's run of a half-hour, stop for a few minutes to walk and stretch, then take two or three brief accelerations to top racing speed. However, if the race is a marathon, stay cool. Take no warmup. Start running—slowly—at the opening gun and use the first few miles to warm up. Starting cool helps you resist the urge most marathoners have to start too fast.

11. *Remember that a little fear is good for you.* It gets the adrenaline pumping, and that will allow you to race farther and faster than you could if you were perfectly calm.
12. *Realize that what you will do today has been predetermined.* Your potential in this race has already been decided before you start. The most accurate predictor is your last racing result. Use the formula in Table 25.1 to project your times from one distance to another.

Table 25.1 *Equal Times*

Performance at one distance accurately predicts potential at another. The slowdown/speedup factor for most runners is about five percent as the distance is doubled or halved. For instance, someone averaging 6:00 per mile for five kilometers would be expected to go five percent slower, or 6:18.

The table lists comparable times for the three most popular racing distances. (All times are rounded to the nearest minute.) It assumes the runner is equally trained for the various distances. Results can be used to measure the effectiveness of training. For example, a 10-K time slower than expected indicates a lack of speed; a faster time signals greater potential in the half-marathon or marathon if endurance is emphasized more.

10-K	Half-Marathon	Marathon
30:00	1:07	2:20
31:00	1:09	2:25
32:00	1:11	2:29
33:00	1:14	2:34
34:00	1:16	2:38
35:00	1:18	2:43
36:00	1:20	2:48
37:00	1:23	2:53
38:00	1:25	2:57
39:00	1:27	3:02
40:00	1:29	3:07
41:00	1:31	3:11

Table 25.1—Continued

10-K	Half-Marathon	Marathon
42:00	1:34	3:16
43:00	1:36	3:20
44:00	1:38	3:25
45:00	1:40	3:30
46:00	1:43	3:34
47:00	1:45	3:39
48:00	1:47	3:43
49:00	1:49	3:48
50:00	1:52	3:52
51:00	1:54	3:57
52:00	1:56	4:01
53:00	1:58	4:06
54:00	2:01	4:10
55:00	2:03	4:15
56:00	2:05	4:19
57:00	2:08	4:24
58:00	2:10	4:28
59:00	2:12	4:33

CHAPTER TWENTY-SIX

The Race

To the runner, a "PR" does not stand for public relations or an island in the Caribbean. It means "personal record," and this PR may represent the greatest advance in the history of this sport.

Traditionally, running picked its winners as all other sports do. The first person to finish won, and everyone else lost. The winner—and only the winner—could add luster to a performance by setting a meet, state, national, or world record.

The invention of the digital stopwatch worn on the wrist turned everyone into a potential winner. Here was a very personal and yet objective way to measure success and progress. It didn't depend upon beating anyone, but only upon how the new numbers on the watch compared with the old ones.

Be proud of your PR, but not so proud that you want to preserve it. Your records, like all records, are made to be broken. No one can break them for you, and no one else can take them from you.

The PR is the only race prize that really means anything. Certificates and T-shirts are awarded to anyone who pays an entry fee, but records must be earned. They don't come to you automatically; they must be won in a race against your former self.

You win the race against time the way all athletes do: by preparing better than this opponent and then racing smarter. You've done the training. Now what can you add to your bag of competitive tricks that will shave extra seconds from the face of that digital watch?

- *Pick your spots.* Race most seriously in the spring or fall, when the weather is likely to be most favorable for fast times (experienced runners prefer a temperature in the fifties). Choose a flat course designated "certified," which indicates that it has passed stringent measurement tests and is certain not to be long or short.
- *Avoid crowds.* Find a race numbering 100 or fewer runners per kilometer (maximum of 1000 in a 10-K; up to about 4000 in a marathon, where they have more distance to spread out). Massive races are human traffic jams which cost you valuable time, while the smaller events allow you to start running at the gun and to follow a straight course.
- *Compete.* Realize that your placing ultimately means nothing, but still use the people in front of you as moving targets. After the starting rush is over and runners up ahead have settled into their pace, reel in one "victim" after another. This helps you without hurting them.
- *Cut corners.* Don't run as if you were driving, always staying in the righthand lane and making proper turns. Race courses are measured along the shortest possible route that a runner could travel, and you penalize yourself by straying from that path.
- Finally, and most importantly, *pace yourself.* Runners hit "walls" because they make one of two mistakes: inadequate training or improper pacing. I'm assuming you've trained well. The set of tables (26.1 to 26.4) in this chapter give general and specific guidelines on pace.

Table 26.1 *Sensible Splits*

The best pace is an even pace. That means saving enough early to allow a strong finish, but not to start so slowly that you can't make up the lost time later. The two halves of the race should fall within a few seconds per mile of equal time.

The "safety margins" below are based on a five-seconds-per-mile factor. Divide both your racing distance and projected time by two, then add and subtract the appropriate amounts to determine what your fastest and slowest halves should be.

For instance, the distance is 10-K and the time goal is forty minutes. The 5-K's should be no faster than 19:29 and no slower than 20:31. If the splits fall outside this range, the race was run inefficiently.

Racing Distance	Halves	Safety Margin
5 kilometers	1.55 miles	plus/minus 16 sec.
8 kilometers	2.5 miles	plus/minus 25 sec.
10 kilometers	3.1 miles	plus/minus 31 sec.
12 kilometers	3.75 miles	plus/minus 38 sec.
15 kilometers	4.15 miles	plus/minus 47 sec.
20 kilometers	6.2 miles	plus/minus 1:02
half-marathon	6.55 miles	plus/minus 1:05
25 kilometers	7.25 miles	plus/minus 1:17
30 kilometers	9.3 miles	plus/minus 1:33
marathon	13.1 miles	plus/minus 2:35
50 kilometers	15.54 miles	plus/minus 2:34

Table 26.2 *Pacing a 10-K*

This commonly run event is a hybrid. Although the full distance is metric, the pace is usually read at *mile* distances. You're advised to run the 10-K at a steady pace, but how do you know what your ideal even-paced racing is? Table 26.2 lists the desired splits at both three miles and 5-K (the approximate and exact halfway points). The ranges of times are based on even pace, minus and plus five seconds per mile. Determine your probable final time, then plan to start no faster or slower than indicated here.

10-K	Per-Mile	3 miles	5 kilometers
30 minutes	4:45 to 4:55	14:16 to 14:46	14:44 to 15:16
31 minutes	4:55 to 5:05	14:45 to 15:15	15:14 to 15:46
32 minutes	5:05 to 5:15	15:14 to 15:44	15:44 to 16:16
33 minutes	5:14 to 5:24	15:43 to 16:13	16:14 to 16:46
34 minutes	5:24 to 5:34	16:13 to 16:43	16:44 to 17:16
35 minutes	5:34 to 5:44	16:41 to 17:11	17:14 to 17:46
36 minutes	5:43 to 5:53	17:10 to 17:40	17:44 to 18:16
37 minutes	5:53 to 6:03	17:39 to 18:09	18:14 to 18:46
38 minutes	6:03 to 6:13	18:08 to 18:38	18:44 to 19:16
39 minutes	6:12 to 6:22	18:38 to 19:07	19:14 to 19:46
40 minutes	6:22 to 6:32	19:06 to 19:36	19:44 to 20:16
41 minutes	6:32 to 6:42	19:35 to 20:05	20:14 to 20:46
42 minutes	6:41 to 6:51	20:04 to 20:34	20:44 to 21:16
43 minutes	6:51 to 7:01	20:33 to 21:03	21:14 to 21:46
44 minutes	7:01 to 7:11	21:02 to 21:32	21:44 to 22:16

Table 26.2—Continued

10-K	Per-Mile	3 miles	5 kilometers
45 minutes	7:10 to 7:20	21:31 to 22:01	22:14 to 22:46
46 minutes	7:20 to 7:30	22:00 to 22:30	22:44 to 23:16
47 minutes	7:30 to 7:40	22:29 to 22:59	23:14 to 23:46
48 minutes	7:40 to 7:50	22:59 to 23:29	23:44 to 24:16
49 minutes	7:49 to 7:59	23:38 to 23:58	24:14 to 24:46
50 minutes	7:58 to 8:08	23:54 to 24:24	24:29 to 25:31
51 minutes	8:08 to 8:18	24:22 to 24:52	24:59 to 26:01
52 minutes	8:17 to 8:27	24:51 to 25:21	25:29 to 26:31
53 minutes	8:26 to 8:36	25:20 to 25:50	25:59 to 27:01
54 minutes	8:36 to 8:46	25:49 to 26:19	26:29 to 27:31
55 minutes	8:46 to 8:56	26:18 to 26:48	26:59 to 28:01
56 minutes	8:55 to 9:05	26:46 to 27:16	27:29 to 28:31
57 minutes	9:05 to 9:15	27:15 to 27:45	27:59 to 29:01
58 minutes	9:14 to 9:24	27:44 to 27:14	28:29 to 29:31
59 minutes	9:25 to 9:35	28:13 to 27:43	28:59 to 30:01

Table 26.3 *Pacing a Half-Marathon*

Because it is rare for a half-marathon race to announce times at the halfway point (6.55 miles), this table lists the desired splits at the common checkpoints of five miles and 10-K. The ranges of times are based upon even pace, minus or plus five seconds per mile. Determine your probable final time, then plan to start no faster or slower than indicated here.

Half Marathon	Per-Mile	5 miles	10 Kilometers
1:10	5:16 to 5:26	26:19 to 27:09	32:37 to 33:39
1:12	5:25 to 5:35	27:04 to 27:54	33:34 to 34:36
1:14	5:34 to 5:44	27:50 to 28:40	34:30 to 35:32
1:16	5:43 to 5:53	28:10 to 29:00	35:27 to 36:29
1:18	5:52 to 6:02	29:21 to 30:11	36:24 to 37:26
1:20	6:01 to 6:11	30:07 to 30:57	37:21 to 38:23
1:22	6:11 to 6:21	30:53 to 31:43	38:18 to 39:20
1:24	6:20 to 6:30	31:39 to 32:29	39:14 to 40:16
1:26	6:29 to 6:39	32:24 to 33:14	40:11 to 41:13
1:28	6:38 to 6:48	33:10 to 34:00	41:08 to 42:10
1:30	6:47 to 6:57	33:56 to 34:46	42:05 to 43:07
1:32	6:57 to 7:07	34:42 to 35:32	43:02 to 44:04
1:34	7:06 to 7:16	35:28 to 36:18	43:58 to 45:00
1:36	7:15 to 7:25	36:13 to 37:03	44:55 to 45:57
1:38	7:24 to 7:34	36:59 to 37:49	45:52 to 46:54
1:40	7:33 to 7:43	37:45 to 38:35	46:49 to 47:51
1:42	7:42 to 7:52	38:31 to 39:21	47:46 to 48:48
1:44	7:51 to 8:01	39:17 to 40:07	48:42 to 49:44
1:46	8:00 to 8:10	40:02 to 40:52	49:39 to 50:41

Table 26.3—Continued

Half Marathon	Per-Mile	5 miles	10 Kilometers
1:48	8:10 to 8:20	40:48 to 41:38	50:36 to 51:38
1:50	8:19 to 8:29	41:35 to 42:25	51:33 to 52:35
1:52	8:28 to 8:38	42:20 to 43:10	52:29 to 53:31
1:54	8:38 to 8:48	43:05 to 43:55	53:26 to 54:28
1:56	8:47 to 8:57	43:53 to 44:43	54:23 to 55:25
1:58	8:57 to 9:07	44:54 to 45:44	57:09 to 58:11

Table 26.4 *Pacing a Marathon*

In shorter races, pacing spells the difference between a faster or slower finish. In the marathon, it may make the difference between finishing and dropping out. This table lists the desired splits at the common checkpoints of ten miles and half-marathon. The ranges of times are based upon even pace, minus or plus five seconds per mile. Determine your probable final time, then plan to start no faster or slower than indicated here.

Marathon	Per-Mile	10 miles	Half-marathon
2:30	5:39 to 5:40	56:25 to 58:05	1:13:55 to 1:16:05
2:35	5:50 to 6:00	58:20 to 1:00:00	1:16:25 to 1:18:35
2:40	6:01 to 6:11	1:00:14 to 1:01:54	1:18:55 to 1:21:05
2:45	6:13 to 6:23	1:02:09 to 1:03:49	1:21:25 to 1:23:35
2:50	6:24 to 6:34	1:04:03 to 1:05:43	1:23:55 to 1:26:05
2:55	6:35 to 6:45	1:05:58 to 1:07:38	1:26:25 to 1:28:35
3:00	6:47 to 6:57	1:07:52 to 1:09:32	1:28:55 to 1:31:05
3:05	6:59 to 7:09	1:09:47 to 1:11:27	1:31:25 to 1:33:35
3:10	7:10 to 7:20	1:11:41 to 1:13:21	1:34:55 to 1:36:05
3:15	7:22 to 7:32	1:13:36 to 1:15:16	1:36:25 to 1:38:35
3:20	7:33 to 7:43	1:15:30 to 1:17:10	1:38:55 to 1:41:05
3:25	7:44 to 7:54	1:17:25 to 1:19:05	1:41:25 to 1:43:35
3:30	7:56 to 8:06	1:19:19 to 1:20:59	1:43:55 to 1:46:05
3:35	8:07 to 8:17	1:21:14 to 1:22:54	1:46:25 to 1:48:35
3:40	8:19 to 8:29	1:23:08 to 1:24:48	1:48:55 to 1:51:05
3:45	8:30 to 8:40	1:25:03 to 1:26:43	1:51:25 to 1:53:35
3:50	8:42 to 8:52	1:26:57 to 1:28:37	1:53:55 to 1:56:05
3:55	8:53 to 9:03	1:28:52 to 1:30:32	1:56:25 to 1:58:35

CHAPTER TWENTY-SEVEN

The Review

Numbers Games

You look up at the overhead clock as you cross the finish line. At the same time, you click off the digital watch on your wrist. You compare the two times and accept the faster.

The first thing you must know when a race ends is, "What was my time?" The second is, "What does it mean?"

Distance and time are objective standards that can make winners of us all. The first victory is finishing. The second is running a distance faster than you have before or faster than expected.

Time for a distance shows more than what happens here and now. Unlike sports with arbitrary scoring systems—football, baseball, tennis, golf, and most others—running results cross lines of time and space. Nebraska's football score against Oklahoma on Saturday tells only what the two teams did against each other that day. It says little about how each might have done against UCLA, or how well they met their own standards of perfection.

Running times transcend these limits. A miler from Nebraska can race against one from Oklahoma today and know how he or she might have done against one from Florida racing someplace else. Not only that, but people racing in 1985 can compete against marks left behind in 1965. This year's runners can leave records for people to break in 2001. Best of all, runners can compete against their own histories and be winners without being first to finish.

Time is your most important result. It not only lets you race this distance with these people; it lets you compare your races with all other races at all distances you have ever or will ever run. This is why you must know your time as you finish. This is why you work out its meanings. It is to be a page in your history.

You have your time. Now start processing it. Get it ready to go into your history book in a form you understand and can compare with earlier and later times.

1. *Compare the time with another known standard.* This race may have been an odd distance, like 7.6 miles. Your time of 52:36 doesn't tell you much, so you reduce it to a minutes-per-mile pace. You divide 52.6 by 7.6. (The figuring is easier if you convert seconds into tenths of a minute.) Your pace was 6.92 minutes or 6:55 per mile. Pace per mile carries more meaning than overall time because you judge all running, training, and racing by this standard. You know immediately after making the per-mile calculations how much faster you raced than you normally run, or how much farther you were able to hold a pace than you do in everyday runs.

2. *Compare the time with your others at this distance.* Times gain meaning as you run standard distances like 10-kilometers, half-marathon, and marathon again and again—or as you race the same course repeatedly. You set personal records and store them in your diary and memory. You break them or know exactly how far you miss them.

3. *Compare this time with those from other events.* You might enter a 10-K race this week, a half-marathon next week and an 8-K a few weeks later. So how do you compare the results from diffferent distances? Start by figuring pace per mile. Then determine a normal slowdown/speedup factor from one distance to another. One method is explained in Table 25.1. You may create a more exact formula for yourself by plotting your best paces for all races on graph paper. From this, you not only can tell instantly if you're faster or slower than expected; you also can predict pace for an unfamiliar distance before you race it.

4. *Compare your projected and actual times for this distance.* These can be taken either from a graph you compile yourself or from the general formula in Table 25.1. A time considerably slower than predicted indicates you have made training errors. Most likely, either the speed or distance training was inadequate. On the other hand, a faster-than-expected time is to be celebrated. Not only did you do well in this race; you probably can expect similar improvement across the board.

5. *Compare your pace for the first and last half of the race.* A dramatic slowdown in the latter stages indicates an overly aggressive start, probably to the detriment of your overall time. A closing rush much faster than the opening means that you probably lost more time early than you could make up. (See Chapter 26 for pacing advice.)

   Two more comparisons are optional. These match you against other runners in a race field. Don't think you have lost if you don't match up well here. The real race is with the distance and your own times.

6. *Compare yourself with everyone else who raced here.* The numbered stick or card you were handed as you finished indicated your overall place. It is only a beginning. You give that number more meaning by turning it into a percentage ranking. Divide your place by the number of starters. For example, you were ninety-eighth of 609. This ranks you in the top sixteen percent. In the next race, you might rank 200th of 2000. The place may be lower, but the rating of ten percent will be better. This system lets you compare accurately the finishes in different-sized events.
7. *Compare yourself with others of your age-group and sex.* In long-distance races, everyone usually starts together, but the results are split into divisions to make up for the inequities between young and old, male and female. See how you rank beside runners like yourself, dividing your group place by the number of its starters to get another percentage.

Clearing the Damage

Racing is as destructive as it is exciting. Don't miss the excitement, but take extreme care in handling the destruction. Recover from the race as if it were an injury that takes time to heal.

The healing period starts or stalls immediately after you finish, depending on how you treat yourself right away. If you stop two steps past the line, stagger to the nearest grassy spot and lie there uncovered for the next hour, you recover slowly. The next few days' runs feel like they've been added onto the end of your race—or worse. But if you keep moving and cool down slowly, the damage done by the race is erased sooner.

The post-race air cools instantly by what seems like twenty degrees. You cool it simply by stopping. That's why you need to put on more clothes than you wore to race. Change to a dry shirt even if the day is warm, jacket and pants if it's cool, and mittens and a cap if it's cold. Resist the temptation to strip next to naked or jump right into a pool in warm weather, or to go right inside from the cold to a hot shower. Either choice invites injury or illness later.

Racing is enough of a shock to the body without subjecting it to such drastic temperature changes. Reserves to fight off illness have already been depleted by the racing effort. You don't need much of an extra jolt to trigger a cold or a case of flu.

Something else is guaranteed if you don't keep moving. Your overworked muscles, saturated with fatigue products, stiffen quickly if you stop suddenly. They have less trouble if you slow them by degrees. Don't sit down immediately. Continue mild exercise in the form of walking, very easy running, or stretching for the next fifteen minutes or so.

What you do on raceday merely begins the healing process. Full recovery takes longer than you might imagine. Runners make the mistake of thinking they are well again once the muscle soreness disappears within a few days. Yet a much deeper and more subtle weariness lingers for many days after a 10-K race and many weeks after a marathon.

Racers (particularly those from the longest distances with extended recovery periods) who jump back into full training and racing before the healing is complete keep the sports doctors busy. Limping into the office a week after the race, the runner complains, "I had no problems in the race, then this happened during yesterday's long run. What bad luck!"

Luck had nothing to do with it. Heaping abuse on a battered body yielded this predictable result.

Jack Foster, who has survived into his fifties as a top-level runner, offers the best rule for clearing away the debris of the race. The New Zealander says he won't allow himself to run hard again until one day has passed for every mile of the race.

This means giving yourself a full week of easy running (no training and certainly no more racing) to get well after a ten-kilometer race, almost a month after the marathon— just to be safe. Recovery recommendations for various racing distances are listed in Table 27.1.

Table 27.1 Race Spacing

Racing is both exciting and risky—exciting during the race, risky afterward. The stress of the race greatly increases the risk of injury. Insure adequate recovery in the post-race period by observing this rule: Do no more hard running until one day has passed for each mile of the race (or at least one week, whichever is longer). The table lists recommended recovery times. Continue normal daily running during this period, but do no serious training or racing.

Racing Distance	Recovery Period
1 mile or 1500 meters	7 days
2 miles or 3 kilometers	7 days
3 miles or 5 kilometers	7 days
5 miles or 8 kilometers	7 days
6 miles or 10 kilometers	7 days
7.5 miles or 12 kilometers	8 days
10 miles or 15 kilometers	10 days
half-marathon or 20 kilometers	14 days
15 miles or 25 kilometers	16 days
20 miles or 30 kilometers	20 days
marathon	27 days
30 miles or 50 kilometers	32 days

THE RUNNING LIFE

Mike Tymn isn't the same person he was seven years ago. Neither are you or me. This is true both physically and emotionally, he says.

Tymn is not only one of the country's better late-forties distance runners; he is one of the nation's better running writers. His columns appear regularly in the *Honolulu Advertiser* and *National Masters News.* He also is one of the few non-academics admitted to a society of sports historians.

Like all good running writers, Tymn wonders why the running boom has quieted and races decreased in size in the mid-1980s. Unlike most other writers, he offers a plausible explanation as to why this happened when it did.

Mike's historical perspective tells him that many types of natural cycles are seven years long. Marriages experience the notorious "seven-year itch" syndrome. Gail Sheehy's best-selling book, *Passages,* identifies major life changes at seven-year intervals. Workers are advised to change jobs every seven years. Farmers worry about swarms of locusts descending on the crops every seven years.

Tymn espouses the intriguing physiological theory that the body completely replaces itself every seven years. No cell in your body today was with you in early 1978. That theory has a psychological companion: the ability to concentrate on a particular activity may also have about a seven-year lifespan.

Knowing these things doesn't exempt Mike from their influences. He complained in 1984 that his racing times weren't improving any more, and he was facing a midlife crisis of sorts. Should he keep pushing, or back off and become a fun/fitness runner? He also saw a connection in the sport as a whole, as other runners faced the same choice: going ahead to more and more organized and serious competition, or settling down into a more relaxed and moderate approach.

Tymn ran in his youth, but he returned to hard training and racing only in the mid-1970s and improved into the eighties. That means he has put in about seven serious years before his times leveled off and he looked for new directions in his running. He went on to say, quite accurately, that running experienced its greatest growth spurt in 1977, as Jim Fixx's book first climbed to the top of the best-seller lists. Seventy-seven plus seven equals eighty-four. . . .

And what happened in 1984? The earlier enthusiasm of the "boom" generation waned as the effects of this seven-year itch were felt. These people looked for changes to make in the way they ran. Some of them quit running, and most of those who remained in the sport started a new cycle that was modified in some way.

I know how they felt. I've passed through several of these cycles. At age seven, I began to dabble in organized sports. At fourteen, I found my sport and began to race seriously on the track. At twenty-one, I switched to semi-serious road racing of marathon length and even longer. At twenty-eight, injuries began to diminish race performances, and I reduced both the training and racing distances. At thirty-five, I became a "fun-racer" who still raced hard occasionally but without the specific preparation needed to race well.

As I write, I'm approaching another probable turning point at age forty-two. I welcome whatever surprising turn it might bring. Each cycle represents an ending and a new beginning. I give something up, but replace it with something at least as good.

CHAPTER TWENTY-EIGHT

The Years

Attitudes on Aging

Satchel Paige pitched major league baseball when his age was somewhere between the late forties and early sixties. He either wasn't sure how old he was or wasn't telling. He coined homespun philosophies that outlived his playing career. He's known best as the man who warned us not to look back; someone might be gaining on us.

Once, when asked the inevitable question about his age, Satch answered with a question of his own: "How old would you be if you didn't know how old you were?"

Think about that. If you didn't know the year you were born, how old would you judge yourself to be by looks and feelings? There is no more accurate test than that. We can't tell by looking at our teeth, as we would with a horse, or by sawing ourselves in half and counting rings, as with a tree.

If you asked me Paige's question, I would say, "It depends. How old *where?*" Like all of us, I'm a man of many ages.

As an athlete, I'm almost ancient. Nearly twenty years ago, someone asked me, "What's an old guy like you doing still running?" And I'm *still* running!

As a writer, I'm almost a child. Everywhere I go to meet readers, someone says, "I expected someone much older"—as if a head of gray hair is one qualification for being published.

My hair is still its original color, but I have perenially sore feet and legs from the pounding I've given them. From the waist down, I feel fifty years old on good days, seventy or eighty on bad ones. From the waist up, I'm told I look ten years younger than my true age.

In many ways, I have more of a teenager's outlook than I did in my teens. I wouldn't let myself be young then. I was too busy trying to grow up fast and acting twice my age. Now, I often act half my age. Then I'm the kid I wouldn't let myself be at twenty.

The calendar puts me just past forty. That much-feared birthday didn't disturb me. The time of mini-crisis was thirty-five. That is a more important landmark on life's journey than forty is. The life expectancy of most Americans is about seventy; thirty-five is the halfway point. It marks the end of growing up and the start of growing old. When we reach the top of this hill, we see for the first time where we're headed—and resist going there.

Gail Sheehy calls the thirty-fifth birthday one of the "predictable crises of adult life." She must be right, because *Passages* struck enough nerves to bcome a best-seller.

After thirty-five, many of the early dreams that haven't come true now look like they never will. The world is seen through glasses, and not rose-colored ones. The lines around the mouth and eyes are deepening, and the skin at the jowls is sagging even on those of us who've stayed lean. The hairline is receding. We can't stay up past midnight any more and expect to greet dawn the next morning with a smile on our lips and a song in our hearts. We have responsibilties, obligations, and worries that cause us to walk more heavily and wearily.

It is not coincidence that so many people take up running in their mid-thirties, or start to train and compete more seriously at that age. Initially it's a way to resist aging; later, it's a means of making peace with that process.

I've made my peace. Not long after the second half began, I saw the plus side of growing older.

- The *pride* of still running well, even though I have more than a few years on me.
- The *wisdom* that comes with experience, and the experience to use wisely what I know.
- The *patience* to let things happen at their own pace rather than trying to make them happen quickly.
- The *assurance* to go my own way, in my own way, at my own rate—without worrying about how other people do things or what they expect of me.
- The *hardness* that comes with absorbing four decades of knocks, and the softness that comes with adjusting to change instead of fighting it.

After the Fad

As longtime runners look around them, they see a once-quiet, once-simple sport that has grown in ways they may not like. Newer runners see they've stumbled onto a good thing, but wonder if it can last. Both groups ask, "Where is running headed?" It's often a worried question, asked out of concern that the sport has taken a wrong turn and is headed for destruction.

Running prospered because it was simple and cheap. A runner didn't need any special skills or settings, didn't need a coach or a team. All he or she needed to start running was a comfortable pair of shoes, open space, and free time.

Running is more complicated now. Its prosperity may have taken away some of the attraction that helped it prosper. It has taken on some of the trappings of a fad or craze in recent years.

Yet when someone tries to tell me it will go the way of the hula hoop or the Twist, I first laugh. Then I say I've been hearing that since 1968, and during that time the running population has exploded.

Finally, I observe that running has three strong forces keeping it going and growing.

1. *It is addictive.* A runner becomes what poet Emily Dickinson called "an inebriate of air." Once you have learned to drink oxygen at eight times the amount you take during a similar period while sitting down, and you feel the cleansing effects this has on you in every way, you're hooked. Few current runners will ever quit.
2. *It is contagious.* Everyone who runs is a carrier. One person sees another run and says, "If he/she can do it, so can I." If every addicted runner infects two more people, think how many runners there will be by the year 2000.
3. *It is hereditary.* Amby Burfoot, a Boston Marathon winner, says his son's first words were, "Mommy run." At two, he already thought it normal and natural for his parents to run every day instead of lighting cigarettes or growing fat. The current generation has made inroads into society's bad habits. The next generation has a running start on good ones simply by imitating elders.

Finally, when someone tells me that running is a fad, I quote Dr. Peter Wood. This researcher with the Stanford Heart Disease Prevention program has run for more than forty years. He writes in his book, *Run to Health:* "If we look at man, we see an animal with powerful legs, clearly designed to run. We see an animal that has effectively used those legs over the centuries, over the evolutionary ages—until some sixty years ago when everyone climbed aboard the automobile, and running became rather quaint except for a few young athletes. From then on, it was all downhill as cars filled the roads, the populace gradually put on weight, and coronary heart disease became first a significant medical problem and finally the greatest health menace of modern times."

Dr. Wood's view: "The 'craze' has been one of *inactivity,* making the running revolution an overdue return to biological sanity."

Olympic marathoner Kenny Moore noticed a return to another kind of sanity before other writers did. He wrote in *Sports Illustrated* several yeas ago of runners rejecting the crowds and hype of the sport's craze phase.

"There are runners now, usually those who have run for years, who no longer come to big races, who feel them to be perverted simply by the crush," Moore said. He predicted that "we may see the stream dividing, one small branch slipping off into the forest."

Time has proven him wrong in only one respect. *Many* streams have branched off. As a growing number of runners return to a quieter approach, these various branches may now hold more people than the old mainstream did. They see that the run can still be a quiet, soothing time—an antidote to the "real world" and not an imitation of it.

Where is running headed? The best answer is another question: "Where is *your* running headed?" That's what matters. None of us has to suffer the whole sport's growing pains. We only have to deal with our own.

The greatest joy in running is the rhythm of my own footsteps as they go down the road each day. Give me two good legs, and a place and time to use them, and I don't need much more.

The Lessons

The Minuses

Garrett Tomczak, a runner from Minnesota with training in philosophy, writes this critique of running literature: "Much as I enjoy most of it, I don't understand the eagerness to print nonsense in defense of the sport. Supposedly objective articles too often come off with that tone of affronted apologetics usually reserved for press releases from the Tobacco Institute."

Anyone who has read anything with my name on it knows that I am an unabashed cheerleader for all that is good in running. If this sport had a Chamber of Commerce, I could serve as its president-for-life.

Still, no one who has spent more than a quarter-century watching the running parade could be blind to its flaws. I see the sport's warts, accept them as inevitable, and share them with you now as a therapeutic exercise.

No runner should become too much of an idealist, because the flipside of idealism is intolerance. We turn sour when we expect our world to be ideal and see so much evidence that it isn't. The way to avoid becoming disillusioned is never to harbor the illusion that running can be perfect.

These are my least-favorite aspects of running.

- Much of the media coverage, which treats running not as a legitimate sport but as a fitness fad and a social phenomenon. At the risk of sounding like an "affronted apologetic," I add that these reports increasingly dwell on the negative side of running without offering a positive balance.
- Articles that describe the men's race first and at greatest length (even when the women ran comparatively better) and which call women "cute," "pretty," or "attractive" while not applying similar adjectives to men.
- Ads that feature models pretending to be runners and that don't fool anyone—certainly not with the sprayed-on "sweat" that forms a too-perfect "V" on their T-shirts.
- Cries from the Rodney Dangerfields of running that they get no respect, are misquoted, or misunderstood, yet who resist being interviewed on the grounds that it intrudes upon their privacy.
- Races that bill themselves as the "next Boston Marathon" or the "next New York," which means they'll never be more than a cheap imitation of Boston or New York. Worse yet are races intent on advertising themselves with an "-est" (longest, toughest, biggest, fastest, hilliest, best)—which indicates that they probably indulge in excesses to become what they claim to be.
- The glorification of post-race beer drinking, treating the running as little more than an excuse to get sloshed. I'm reminded of alcohol's cost every time I pass the stone wall in Eugene where Steve Prefontaine crashed his sports car and died.
- The implication that triathloning has taken over ground once held by road running and has become a haven for disenchanted marathoners. The triathlon is still one-third running. Triathletes must continue to train as runners, and they probably will remain runners after their fascination with the new sport wears off.
- Running in the dark. Running on dirty, sloppy, or crusty snow. Slipping into shoes still clammy from yesterday's run. The first mile of an early-morning run that comes less than an hour after sleep.
- Passing through the lobbies of classy hotels to go running, wearing only shorts and a T-shirt, amid crowds of well-dressed business people; or returning from a warm-weather run and riding in an elevator crowded with fellow passengers who move as far from me as the enclosed space will allow.
- Drivers who treat runners as unwelcome intruders and won't yield an inch of road space, forcing a retreat to the relative safety of the gutter; runners who claim the middle of a traffic lane as their territory and won't budge from it, putting themselves and drivers at risk; dog owners who shout, "He won't hurt you," as the pet attacks.
- Pedestrians who ask for directions or time. They mean no harm but make me feel foolish. My brain is on automatic and barely knows where I am, let alone how to get someplace else. My wristwatch isn't programmed to tell the time of day.
- Watches that beep a cadence. What runners do to waste their own money and spoil the tranquility of their own runs is their business. But when they wear a beeper in a race, their noise pollution becomes an irritant to everyone within earshot.

- "Tailgating" runners who fall into step behind me, refusing either to drop back or to pass, as if the morning run were an Olympic 10,000 final.
- Offering a friendly greeting to another runner on the road, and being ignored or glared at in return. This makes me wonder if this once-friendly sport has turned as cold and hostile as a city street.
- People who complain too much about the few things wrong with the sport instead of appreciating all that is right.

The Plusses

A sad result of Jim Fixx's death is the impression left with the general public that he lived a lie and died in vain. Since July 20th, 1984, every runner has been challenged with the question, "If running is so good for you, why didn't it save Fixx?"

The best answer is that Jim didn't run primarily to save his life or to extend it, nor do most of us. He may have started running out of concern for his heart. But he soon discovered, as we have, the more positive benefits that *kept* him running.

Fixx knew, as we do, that running is less a physical act than a mental and emotional exercise. The physiological results are less immediate and dramatic than the psychological ones. Those could be found in other activities, even sedentary ones, that provide the time to be creative and a chance to be heroic.

Creative. The "loneliness of the long-distance runner" is a myth that confuses being alone with being lonely. Runners look forward to the aloneness of a run. Running gives you the chance to take charge of your own actions and thoughts. You alone choose the distance and pace. You leave behind the crowd and its conventions. You put distance between yourself and the publications that bring you other people's thoughts. You escape the packaged voices of radio, TV, and stereo. You get away from the phone, which can interrupt you at any other time.

For up to an hour a day, you take full command of and responsibility for what you do and think. It is your quietest and calmest and most productive hour. That's when you make friends with yourself and prepare to go back into the crowd on more peaceful terms.

Not everyone needs to run. But everyone deserves that one hour in every twenty-four to make something that is his or hers alone.

Much of life is now defined by what you *have:* job, house, address, degree, title, clothes, car. None of that counts when you run. You're stripped down to what you *are:* a body and a mind facing the elements of time, distance, and environment. The pleasures you get from a run are both free and priceless. You can have them any day, but no amount of money can buy them. Only effort can.

The road and the runner's body are like a painter's canvas and brush, a writer's paper and pen, a sculptor's marble and chisel. They are common raw materials—nothing until the artist makes something of them. Anyone can pick up the materials, but only special care can transform them into art.

Art has been defined as "an uncommon thing made from common materials." An artist is one who brings order and beauty to the random, chaotic events of his or her life, and who sees common things is uncommon ways.

By these definitions, runners are artists who find value in the simplest of acts, who make the best pieces of art from materials they have available at the moment. This has nothing to do with the new Mercedes or the battered 1969 Volkswagen they might drive, or whether they wear an "M.D." after their name or have their names on the unemployment rolls.

No one can buy artistic talent, but anyone can produce art.

Heroic. Knowing how small you are helps you grow up, and running can always generate ways to reduce the size of your ego. No matter how many steps you have behind you, you're never more than one away from disaster. You learn in every bad run and every failed race that this sport can humble those who think they have all the answers.

Running can also make the most humble of us feel like a hero. Winning races isn't reserved for the person who finishes first overall or for those who place first in their divisions. Everyone who races can be a winner.

That doesn't mean, however, that you automatically win by racing. If you did, your "victories" wouldn't mean anything. This sport, like all sports, carries the risk of losing. But this one, unlike most others, gives everyone an equal chance to win. That's because its standards are both objective and personal. You don't have to measure yourself against other competitors: only against distance and time. You don't have to beat anyone else to win; you have only to better your own records.

"I have found my hero, and I am he/she" is almost a cliche in running now. But it's still a rare idea in sports as a whole and rarer still in the outside world. Most people still have a hero instead of being one. Most of them rank themselves, or let themselves be ranked, against everyone else doing what they do. Most let themselves think in terms of what they *can't* do and not what they can. Most never let themselves be proud of themselves.

You need something you do yourself that makes you proud—even if it is only to run a mile farther or a minute faster than before. You need something no one else can do for you.

The Friends

Early Heroes

"Who were your first running heroes?" an interviewer asked.

"Anyone my size," I answered immediately. No one ever made bigger heroes out of smaller men than I did when I was a kid.

My first heroes were Johnny Kelley and Albie Thomas. Kelley won the 1957 Boston Marathon and made two U.S. Olympic teams. Thomas, an Australian, set world two- and three-mile records, and ran a 3:58 mile in the summer of 1958.

Their performances impressed me, but not nearly so much as their dimensions. My first heroes both stopped growing at five-feet-six and 130 pounds, as I did. Johnny and Albie—even their nicknames were those of little people. They looked like me and gave me hope that I might run like them.

Small as Kelley and Thomas were, they were giants in my eyes. I worshipped these heroes from afar, by way of *Track and Field News* and *Long Distance Log*. I never saw either of them run in person or even on television, never wrote either of them a fan letter. When we met twenty years later, I approached them shyly, almost reluctantly—partly in awe, partly fearing that my longtime idols would have feet of clay.

Johnny Kelley had come west from Connecticut to speak at a *Runner's World* event. I sat in the audience not to see bigger people, such as world marathon record-holders Grete Waitz and Derek Clayton, but to look up and listen to my old hero.

Kelley still looked quite fit, at least a decade younger than his fifty years—a scale-model John F. Kennedy in both appearance and accent. Kelley spoke modestly but well about his running then and now. I knew I had picked the right hero all those years ago.

After the talk, a friend caught me as I was leaving. "Someone wants to meet you," he said. "Wait here while I get him." I couldn't imagine who would want to meet me at this celebrity-crowded event.

The friend came back leading the reddish-haired little man I'd just heard speak. I would have bolted for the door if Johnny Kelley hadn't already seen me and if the crowd wasn't blocking my escape route.

We both acted embarrassed during introductions. Then we sat down to talk, and we quickly relaxed as the discussion reached common ground.

The man who'd brought us together later told me, "You don't know how hard it was to get you and Kelley together. He was really nervous about meeting you."

It seemed that in the last few years Johnny, an English teacher, had worked on his writing. I'd read his published material and liked it. Little wonder. I learned that he had used my work as a model. My hero had made something of a hero out of me. Imagine that!

Kelley and I talked about this, then laughed about it. There no longer was any awe standing between us. Each bit of hero-worship canceled out the other, and we came to treat each other as friends and equals.

About that same time, I traveled to Chicago. As we drove into the city from the airport, my host said, "You're sharing the house with Al Thomas."

"Oh, where's Al from?" I said with only vague interest. I figured he was a runner from Peoria or Fort Wayne.

"Australia."

"Albie Thomas! *The* Albie Thomas?" I asked. I feared how I would act around him, that I would turn into a tongue-tied kid again.

"I'm in the sha-uh." The Aussie-accented voice came from the bathroom as we entered the apartment. "Shower," I think he said.

Thomas came out a few minutes later. Even though I knew his height as well as my own, I expected someone seven feet tall and dressed like royalty. Thomas wore only a towel, and I was surprised at being able to look him in the eyes.

I turned formal during introductions, saying, "It's an honor to meet you, Mr. Thomas."

"Just call me Albie," he said with an embarrassed wave. "You mike me feel awld with that mistuh stuff."

Our host then left us alone, my worst fear. We began talking, and I took care to stay on the safe ground of present and recently past events. We talked about things runners always talk about: training, the race at hand, shoes, injuries, the weather. I finally admitted to Albie how I'd once idolized him and how much he had meant to my early career.

He shrugged off the compliment, saying, "That was a long time ago. Now I run for fun just like you do."

By the time we went out for dinner, I realized I wasn't in awe of him any more. I'd lost a hero from twenty years earlier and gained a friend. Of the two, I much prefer to have—and to be—the latter.

Lasting Friendships

"In a cold world, you need your friends to keep you warm." So read the advertising slogan of the movie *The Big Chill*.

Running isn't far removed from that cold world. Many of us who have been around the circuit for a while sometimes think this sport has grown chilly and impersonal. That's when we most need our friends to warm us.

I can't remember a story that gave me a warmer feeling than one I did on the friends who helped me launch my book-writing career. Six of us contributed to *LSD: The Humane Way to Train* in 1969. I'm pleased to have known them since the 1960s, pleased to have arranged a reunion in print on the fifteenth anniversary of that book's publication. I was moved by the one conclusion we all seemed to have reached separately: Now more than ever before, we don't and can't run alone.

You might say that retelling these runners' stories is a nostalgic exercise. That's partly true. But the article that we wrote together is also evidence that we hadn't stood still. This was a record of changes that go far beyond these six, changes that are sport-wide and even society-wide.

Simply put, I see a warming trend setting in. Long gone are the strident voices of revolt from the 1960s, when everyone seemed driven to protest everything established and traditional. Fading is the do-my-own-thing-and-ignore-everyone-else independence of the 1970s, the so-called "Me Decade." The 1980s might come to be known as the "Us Decade," as we look again to friends for comfort.

Whatever the reason, I now receive an unusual number of phone calls and letters from old friends wanting to link past with present. Some of them reflect on the 1960s as a paradise lost.

Jon Hendershott, a fellow junior editor at *Track and Field News* in the late sixties, writes that "running is far more complicated than it used to be. Both of us can remember the days when all we had to worry about was lacing our shoes comfortably and making certain our nylon shorts were right-side out. Just go out and run—no need to worry about pronation, runner's nipple, or the myriad of concerns that runners today seem to have. Like so many other things, running was somehow simpler then."

Hendershott's most telling comment: "We all shared the same common ground then—running for the sake of running."

We who were there still share that ground as we talk about it now among ourselves. We tell the new generation of runners, if they care to listen, that they can take their running as simply and joyously and personally as we did ours.

To one degree or another, the six runners who contributed to the *LSD* book have all stepped outside ourselves. We all now say that the running experience grows richer by far when we can share it with people who know what we're talking about.

Three of the six teach running full-time, and another does it part-time. Amby Burfoot and I report the sport for a living, and Tom Osler moonlights as a writer and lecturer.

But it is Ed Winrow, a coach at Mansfield University in Pennsylvania, who communicates most directly with the next generation of runners. More than any of us, Winrow realizes that no one learns alone and that we should give full credit to our teachers.

Each of us can, in retrospect, point to someone we'll always thank for setting our early course. I freely admit that few of my ideas are original. I see myself as a relay runner, passing important messages from the giants who came before me to the people who follow. These exchanges are as satisfying as the best of my races ever were.

Osler agrees. He says, "The opportunity to meet runners and discuss our sport is a great pleasure. Through seminars and letters, I am able to learn how other runners find my ideas."

For Bob Deines, the passing of information is more personal. He lists as a high point of his career "seeing my father get involved in running. At age sixty-seven, he ran his first half-marathon."

Jeff Kroot reflects fondly on his "golden age" as a runner—a time when, he says, "I knew my competitors, and we had thrilling races." He believes that sense of competition, the kind that drew out his best efforts, has almost disappeared in faceless crowds of today's megaraces.

It may take some looking, but the people who make the races personal and the sport friendly are still here. Finding them and staying in contact is worth the effort.

Index